Minimum Wages and Social Policy

Minimum Wages and Social Policy

Lessons from Developing Countries

Wendy V. Cunningham

 **THE WORLD BANK**

1818 H Street NW
Washington DC 20433
Telephone: 202-473-1000
Internet: www.worldbank.org
E-mail: feedback@worldbank.org

ISBN-10:	0-8213-7011-1
ISBN-13:	978-0-8213-7011-7
eISBN-10:	0-8213-7012-X
eISBN-13:	978-0-8213-7012-4
DOI:	10.1596/978-0-8213-7011-7

Cover art: *Construction Workers*, 1976 woodcut, by Vernal Reuben, Jamaica. World Bank Art Collection 466540. Reproduced by permission of Susan Reuben and with assistance from the World Bank Art Program.

Library of Congress Cataloging-in-Publication Data

Cunningham, Wendy V.
    Minimum wages and social policy : lessons from developing countries / Wendy V. Cunningham.
    p. cm.
Includes bibliographical references.
ISBN-13: 978-0-8213-7011-7
ISBN-10: 0-8213-7011-1
ISBN-10: 0-8213-7012-X (electronic)
1. Minimum wage—Latin America. 2. Social policy—Latin America. I. Title.

HD4920.L38C86 2007
331.2'3098—dc22   2007003319

Contents

Boxes

Figures

Tables

Acknowledgments

The report was prepared with inputs from a team of professionals. Special recognition is deserved by the team who wrote the background papers: Carlos Arango, Rolando Guzman, Nicolai Kristensen, Magdalena Lizardo, Dayna Lora, Naercio Menezes Filho, David Neumark, Angela Pinchon, Laura Ripani, and Lucas Siga. Andres Lopez and Laura Saenz provided research assistance for the entire report. The process of report development greatly benefited from the technical inputs, debates, and direction provided by Ariel Fiszbein, William Maloney, Jorge Moreno, Carolina Sanchez-Paramo, Sergei Soares, Francisco Carneiro, Mauricio Santamaria, Luis Serven Diez, Guillermo Perry, Helena Ribe, and Jennie Litvack. Of course, all views presented and errors herein are the sole responsibility of the author.

Introduction

The minimum wage is an attractive policy tool for poverty reduction and social justice. It does not require significant direct government expenditures, is a simple and visible way for the government to show its commitment to social justice and support those at the bottom of the income distribution, is easily targeted to the poorest workers, and affects a market—the labor market—in which Latin American governments are comfortable intervening. Other social programs with poverty reduction objectives have been tried, such as cash transfers or public works, but they tend to be difficult to target and monitor, impose high nonlabor costs, and create political economy disputes. Thus, the self-targeting, lower monitoring, low leakage, "right" worker incentive and labor market–focused characteristics of the minimum wage may make it an attractive social protection tool.

The minimum wage was created in the late 19th century in New Zealand and Australia, and within 30 years it had a strong presence in Latin America and the Caribbean (LAC). The design of LAC's minimum wage institutions was based on two principal objectives. The fair wage objective[1] centered on the idea that each occupation has a fair wage, which may be different from the level determined by the market. Ideally, collective bargaining would correct the imbalance, but if that was not possible, it was the government's responsibility to set and enforce the wage structure by creating occupation-specific wages so that each worker received his or her relative due wage. The poverty alleviation objective was based on the idea that market wages would not necessarily be at a level that was socially acceptable to society, so the minimum wage would ensure enough income for all citizens to maintain a minimum standard of living, regardless of occupation. Over time, the role of the minimum wage in LAC continued to develop to meet the changing economic and social needs in the Region, resulting in a heterogeneous mix of institutions today.

Despite the long history of the minimum wage, very little is known about its effectiveness in meeting its social justice or poverty alleviation roles. Although it may increase consumption by elevating wages above their market level, it may also lead to job loss (through layoffs) and decreased consumption. Thus, its usefulness for poverty and inequality reduction is uncertain. Similarly, in the social justice context, an exogenously imposed wage structure may be a means of overcoming unfair market allocations of wages, but the market will still drive labor demand, and higher-than-market wages may lead to unemployment. This begs the question of how the minimum wage can be designed to be an effective tool to ensure social justice or poverty alleviation.

The literature in the United States and western Europe shows that the minimum wage has modest impacts on wages and employment (mostly with respect to youth), with few poverty or inequality impacts, but there are many reasons to think that the effects on wages, employment, and household income in LAC may differ from those in the Organisation for Economic Co-operation and Development (OECD). Relative to the OECD, LAC has very large informal sectors in which labor laws are not enforced, a greater proportion of adults who earn very low wages and thus may be affected by a minimum wage, incomplete social safety nets for counterbalancing the negative effects of the minimum wage, and a frequent practice of linking the minimum wage to government expenditures. Thus, minimum wages in LAC may affect different sectors of the population and have higher impacts on household welfare and public finance than in the United States and Europe.

Although the minimum wage exists in every country in the LAC Region, there is very little research on the wage and employment effects of the minimum wage and even less on the poverty and household inequality effects. This is particularly troubling, since the minimum wage is a very active policy tool—renegotiated regularly—and labor markets are particularly sensitive to the negative impacts of excessive labor market regulations (Heckman and Pages 2004). Currently, governments across the region are rethinking their social protection systems to make them more integrated and cohesive, so this is an ideal time to empirically sort out the impacts of the minimum wage in LAC and provide policy makers with new information on this policy tool.

Minimum Wage Debates in the Region

Policy makers have been pondering the question of how the minimum wage can be used as a social protection tool. Several issues are being debated in the LAC Region today regarding minimum wages:

- *Is the minimum wage an effective poverty reduction tool?* Throughout the Region, the minimum wage is believed to benefit the poor. In many countries, it served as a benchmark to protect the poor during hyper-inflationary periods, and it is still debated regularly when the (semi-) annual adjustments to the minimum wage are made. These debates are largely speculative, with little empirical evidence to back them up.

- *Do minimum wages exacerbate the unemployment situation?* Throughout the Region, unemployment is an increasing problem. In these market economies, an above-market wage is expected to create unemployment, so the question is how high can the government set the wage without exacerbating unemployment?

- *Are minimum wage policies a means to increase low wages?* As the economies of LAC open to the world, and as highly skilled labor becomes more valuable, the wage gap between skilled and unskilled workers is increasing. Returns to education—one of the principal factors in wage determination—among the most skilled are very high (nearly 20 percent for some countries) and increasing, whereas the returns are much lower, and stagnant, among the less skilled, thus leading to increasing wage inequality and the problems that accompany it.[2] Clearly, an increase in education and investments in technology are the long-run solution, but in the short run, wage policies may be useful to control inequality.

- *Are minimum wage policies effective in economies with a large informal sector?* Informal sector workers earn the lowest wages and are therefore the group most in need of wage protection. However, informal sector workers are by definition outside the government's sphere of direct influence, so minimum wage policies may skip over exactly the group that they are intended to benefit.

- *Can the minimum wage offer labor protection to vulnerable groups?* Youth unemployment is a grave concern in LAC. Minimum wages are thought to deter labor force entry of young individuals, since young people's marginal productivity may be lower than the minimum wage. Thus, discussions about the need to waive the minimum wage for young people through a subminimum apprenticeship wage is being tested in countries as diverse as St. Vincent and the Grenadines and Colombia and is being discussed in other countries in the region. However, others argue that the minimum wage *should* be above the marginal productivity of young workers to give them the incentive to remain in school rather than join the labor market. The increasing spread between the wages of low- and high-skilled workers is also becoming a concern, particularly with trade liberalization.

- *What is the cost of the minimum wage to the public deficit?* Minimum wages are tied to social programs in many LAC countries, so changes in the minimum wage may exacerbate deficit issues. Furthermore, the large public sector in some countries, the increasingly troublesome pension deficit, and increasing or stubborn poverty lead to much wider consequences from minimum wage increases.

The Objective of the Report and Methodology

This report contributes to the debate by attempting to better understand the distributional effects of the minimum wage and thus its usefulness as a policy tool for reducing poverty and inequality. It does not discuss whether or not minimum wage policies should exist. Instead, it assumes that minimum wages will continue to be a part of social policy and presents new research useful to policy makers in designing the minimum wage and the accompanying larger social policy.

The study begins with the existing literature on minimum wages in the Region, but expands the discussion in three ways. First, the household is placed at the center of the debate. Although it is important to understand the employment and wage effects of minimum wages, ultimately we are interested in the general equilibrium effects at the level of the household, which is the unit of observation for poverty measurement. This report presents new research that allows for risk pooling at the household level, where the net implications of job loss and income can be quantified. Second, new research is presented on how the minimum wage affects groups whose labor market participation and success is considered "vulnerable," that is, youth, women, the low-skilled, and informal sector workers. Third, the report provides new discussions on the implications of the minimum wage for state finances by moving beyond the pension issue and into questions of the public wage bill and indexing of social benefits to the minimum wage.

Whereas much of the information presented in this report is drawn from the existing literature, additional information was created to round out the lessons. Specifically, six background papers that apply the latest methodologies from U.S. and European literature to data from the Region were commissioned for this study. The results of the papers are discussed in this study, and the methodologies are presented in appendix I. Particular attention is given to the unique characteristics of LAC, which may differentiate the research findings from those in the United States and Europe, where most minimum wage research has been done. This requires treating the formal and informal sectors separately and allowing for minimum wage effects beyond the low-wage population.

Although this is a Regional study, a caveat is in order. The results are presented for LAC, although every country is not discussed. General information is presented for most countries in the Region, but a subset of countries is selected for deeper analysis that could provide wide-reaching lessons. Mexico, Brazil, and Colombia provide results for countries where the minimum wage is low, medium, and high, respectively, relative to unskilled wages.[3]

Report Organization

The report has eight sections following this introduction. Chapter 2 presents a history of the minimum wage in LAC, the theory behind the functioning of the minimum wage, and empirical evidence from the OECD to lay a foundation for the Latin American experience. Chapter 3 presents an overview of the minimum wage in the Region, including a discussion of the definition of a minimum wage, institutional design, and who earns it. Chapter 4 focuses on the worker; it summarizes the existing literature, presents new evidence on the wage and employment effects of a minimum wage, and gives special attention to "vulnerable" labor market groups. Chapter 5 turns its attention to the household and presents the new (and only) evidence on the effects of the minimum wage on household poverty and inequality in LAC. Chapter 6 considers the state and discusses the cost of minimum wages to the government. Chapter 7 opens the discussion to the rest of the world and considers the lessons learned in other countries about setting, managing, and enforcing the minimum wage. Finally, chapter 8 concludes and presents policy considerations. Specific details about research methodologies and regression results are given in appendix I.

Notes

1. Since 1999, the International Labour Organization (ILO) has argued that the fair wage concept should be the basis for minimum wage regimes.

2. High wage inequality is associated with higher levels of violence (as the have-nots are increasingly faced with the wealth that they do not have), political discord, and the creation of two societies, side by side, with different levels of development (Fajnzylber et al. 1999).

3. In addition, these countries have long enough (noninflationary) time series and sufficient variance in the minimum wage over the period of the data to permit in-depth analysis.

CHAPTER 1

Overview

Introduction

The minimum wage originated as a social justice tool to provide socially acceptable wages to the most unskilled workers. By the time it was adopted in Latin America, it had become more generous, guaranteeing a wage that would allow for a good life for a worker and his or her family, including adequate food, shelter, clothing, hygiene, and leisure. However, economic theory points out that setting a wage above its market value will lead to unemployment, primarily among the most unskilled workers—precisely those the minimum wage is intended to protect. Thus, the question for policy makers is how a minimum wage policy can ultimately help or hurt the poorest workers. Despite widespread debate over the appropriate level and design of the minimum wage throughout the region, there is surprisingly little empirical evidence on its actual impact.

This report examines how minimum wages affect the income poverty of workers, their households, and the state. It does not question whether or not the minimum wage is a good policy: instead, it focuses on the trade-offs in setting the minimum wage level. It takes as a starting point the literature on the wage and employment effects of minimum wages in Latin America and expands the discussion in three ways. First, the household is placed at the center of the debate. Poverty and inequality are measured at the level of the household, rather than at the individual level, to allow for employment and wage trade-offs among individuals who pool their income. Employing recently introduced statistical techniques, this study is the first that uses estimated, rather than simulated, measures of the effect of the minimum wage on household poverty and inequality in the Region.[1] Second, new research is presented on how the minimum wage affects groups whose labor market participation and success is considered "vulnerable": that is, youth, women, the low-skilled, and informal sector workers. Third, the implications of the minimum wage on wage and social expenditures of the government are measured. In the end, the report argues that the minimum wage by itself is not a sufficient tool for protecting the income of the poorest households, and that other social protection tools are necessary to complement it.

Report Findings

Minimum wage policies matter in Latin America and the Caribbean (LAC), unlike the United States or western Europe. A large fraction of the labor force in Latin America and the Caribbean is not covered by minimum wage laws since these persons work in the informal sector. Among those covered, the minimum wage is often not enforced, partly because of weak institutions. Despite these facts, the minimum wage appears to have a larger effect than expected for two reasons, as follows:

(a) Both formal and informal sector workers' salaries are affected by the minimum wage. In fact, the minimum wage is *more binding in the informal than the formal sector*. This may be due to supply- or demand-side factors. On the supply side, the minimum wage is considered a "fair wage" in the economy, regardless of sector. On the demand side, even informal sector employers will voluntarily offer the fair wage to attract labor and minimize labor turnover.

(b) The effects are felt by a larger fraction of the labor force than just minimum wage earners. Only youth in the OECD, whose wages are clustered around the minimum wage, benefit from minimum wage increases. In Latin America and the Caribbean, wage gains are largest for those earning near the minimum wage, but the *wage benefits (and job losses) are experienced throughout the entire wage distribution*.

The minimum wage can be a tool for poverty and inequality reduction. Although the minimum wage falls below the poverty line in households with a single worker, it can serve to increase the incomes of the poorest workers. In countries with relatively low minimum wage levels, it increases the wages of poorer workers, has minimal effects on unemployment, and leads to an aggregate net increase in household labor income for the poor households. It also reduces income inequality because the positive impacts shrink to zero in higher-earning households.

The minimum wage can be set so that it leads to greater income inequality. However, in countries with relatively high minimum wages, the minimum wage can increase wages of higher earners, increase unemployment among the poor, cause greater poverty among the poor, and cause an increase in household labor income inequality. Thus, whereas a high minimum wage may serve a social justice objective, setting it too high can have the opposite effect.

The most vulnerable workers are the first to be hurt by high minimum wages. Even where minimum wages are relatively low, they disproportionately affect certain groups in the labor market. The wages of young, low-skilled, and female workers benefit from a higher minimum wage—as do those of prime-aged, skilled, and male workers—but the unemployment effects are also concentrated on the former groups. In essence, their income is redistributed to less vulnerable segments of the labor force when the minimum wage increases.

Social justice is costly to public finances. Social expenditures are closely tied to the minimum wage throughout Latin America and the Caribbean, so any increase in the minimum wage also has large implications for the public deficit. The largest expenditure category affected is the public sector wage bill. For example, a 10 percent increase in the minimum wage would increase total government expenditure by 1.4 percent in Panama. However, high costs come through tying the minimum wage to other social benefits. For example, in Brazil, a 10 percent increase in the minimum wage would increase pension payouts by 3.3 times more than the increase in receipts.

Issues for Policy Discussion

Careful thought should be given to the structure of minimum wage institutions to enable their use as effective policy tools. Simply having a minimum wage is not sufficient to cause or prevent poverty reduction and income equality. Instead, it is a tool that must be carefully calibrated—in the context of other institutions, norms, values, and constraints of the economy and a society—to reach policy makers' objectives. The most important dimensions for development of an effective minimum wage are as follows:

Clear objective. The minimum wage has played roles ranging from poverty reduction to macroeconomic stabilization. It cannot be a cure-all for society's problems; it is most effective if it has a focused role and if the institution is designed to fulfill this role.

Simple structure. The least effective minimum wage institutions are those that are too complex to be effective. A clear objective will simplify the design of the minimum wage institutions, but even within this, it is better to design a simple system that is well understood by all, rather than trying to fully address the heterogeneous needs of the labor force. A system should have only as many minimum wages as it can enforce, and all criteria should be well defined. It is also crucial to delink the minimum wage from other policies that affect public finance so that minimum wage decisions are independent from public finance issues or from other social decisions.

Enforceable. Although there is a degree of self-enforcement of the minimum wage in Latin America, and clear objectives and a simple structure will facilitate this, it is still necessary to create incentives so that the policy will be followed. This requires setting a wage that is sensitive to the impact on employers; identifying, publicizing, and enforcing punishments for lack of compliance; clearly identifying who is responsible for enforcement of each minimum wage (for example, if the minimum wage differs by occupation, region, or demographic group, it is best if specific bodies, whether unions, regional offices, or advocacy groups, watch over the enforcement of their respective minimum wage); and adequately funding and supporting the administrative body responsible for enforcement.

Set at a level that balances social goals and market responses to minimum wage. A minimum wage that is too high may actually *increase* poverty, so social justice guidelines are not sufficient to set a minimum wage. Similarly, the market may recommend wages that are too low to be acceptable by society. A careful balance must therefore be struck between the objectives. Clear guidelines have not been identified, primarily because the social expectations and the market reaction to a certain value of a minimum wage will differ across countries. Instead, trial and error with high-quality impact evaluation will define a set of parameters for accurate minimum wage setting in the context of each country.

The minimum wage may cause unemployment, so there is a need to combine it with other social welfare tools. Whereas a well-targeted policy of tax and redistribution would most efficiently achieve the income inequality reduction objective, the minimum wage may be a more realistic means for achieving this goal. It avoids many of the pitfalls of other social policies: self-targeting, market (rather than government) income redistribution, minimal public administration, no perverse labor supply incentives (receipt of benefit is contingent on being in the labor force), and it does not ring of paternalism (*asistencialismo*) or political favoritism (*clientelismo*), as the beneficiaries are selected by the market. However, minimum wages can cause unemployment, particularly among the most vulnerable workers. Thus, a minimum wage that is high enough to affect wages should be accompanied by a tax-and-redistribute scheme that reallocates income from all workers—not just the poor, as in the case of the minimum wage—to the poor who lose their jobs as a result of the policy.

Note

1. The research on the household poverty effects of the minimum wage is scarce in the Organisation for Economic Co operation and Development (OECD) literature as well. In the Latin America Region, there exists research that simulates the poverty effects of the minimum wage and examines the "poverty" of the individual as a result of the minimum wage, but both are based on strong assumptions that may drive their results.

CHAPTER 2

Context and Framework

The historical development of minimum wage institutions and the theoretical underpinning provide a context for deeper analysis of the tool. The brief review in this chapter is not intended to be comprehensive. Rather, it demonstrates the high expectations countries have for the tool and that under fairly plausible conditions, the minimum wage may have a more limited effect (or even the reverse) than that hoped for. The OECD literature is also reviewed, exposing its limitations for understanding the LAC situation. Theoretical ambiguity about the impact of the minimum wage makes the empirical work presented in this study critical to formulating minimum wage policy.

The Historical and Social Justice Perspective—Birth and Evolution of the Minimum Wage

The minimum wage was created in the late 19th century in response to public demands for social justice among workers.[1] The objective was to alleviate the situation of "sweating," defined as working at wages so low that they did not support "a socially acceptable level of wholesome family life" (Nordlund 1997). The low wages were attributed to the failure of a competitive market to offer an adequate wage level and the lack of bargaining power by the most vulnerable workers, namely women, children, and the unskilled. Or, as stated by the English economist, Sidney Webb, who is credited with coining the term "sweating" (Webb 1912):

> Experience has demonstrated, to the satisfaction of public opinion, as well as of economists, that to leave the determinants of wages, in a capitalist organization or industry, to the unfettered operation of "individual bargaining" and the "haggling of the market" between individual employers and individual wage-earners, is to produce, in the community, a large area of "sweating"— defined by the House of Lords Committee of 1890 as "earnings barely sufficient to sustain existence."

The original proponents of the minimum wage argued that low wages impose substantial negative externalities on society, and that government has a responsibility to correct the market and serve as a collective bargaining proxy for poor workers without representation to ensure them a standard of living acceptable to society. Early court cases show that despite the unconstitutionality of minimum wages in some countries, and legal suits by workers against the minimum wages (because of their adverse employment effects—see box 2.1), public pressure slowly won as minimum wages were instituted across the world.

Latin America was one of the leaders in instituting minimum wages, but the policy objective differed from that of the originators.[2] After World War II, many Latin American countries began to adopt detailed legislation to socially engineer the labor markets in response to the population's expectation that the government was responsible for their well-being and that markets were not able to produce the socially desirable results (Starr

---

Box 2.1

Employees *against* High Minimum Wages?

The wage-employment trade-off of the minimum wage can lead employees to fight the government to lower minimum wages. For example, in 1923 in the United States, the Supreme Court ruled on the case *Adkins v. Children's Hospital* (chi. 8.88), in which a group of women sued the District of Columbia to halt the implementation of a minimum wage that had led to their losing their jobs. The court ruled in favor of the prosecution, stating that the minimum wage was a form of price fixing and an unreasonable infringement on individuals' freedom to choose the price at which they would sell their services.

1993). Constitutions and legislation specified that wages should be sufficient to provide for food, shelter, clothing, transport, leisure, and other basic necessities of life. Thus, the motivation for a minimum wage was partly social justice and partly to affect the wage distribution in order to offer "fair" wages (see box 2.2 for other motivations).

Box 2.2

The Motivation for the Creation of Minimum Wages

The rationale for creation of a minimum wage varied across country, time, pressure group, and institutions. Some of the motivations included the following:

Protection of the most vulnerable. This was the early objective of the minimum wage, where those with the least bargaining power and the most inhumane living standards were the target of the policy.

Poverty reduction. Linked to the concept of protection of the most vulnerable, this objective identifies the "most vulnerable" as the poor and argues for a single minimum wage that allows a basic standard of living for all citizens.

Payment for inputs. Early court cases in the United States argued that employers are obligated to pay for the production of the human energy required to supply the labor to their firms. Thus, wages should be sufficient to cover the cost of food, shelter, leisure, clothing, and other inputs that create labor. A minimum wage should be equal to this cost, and it would be unjust for employers to pay a lower wage.

Fair labor standards. The International Labor Organization (ILO) 1919 charter argued that all occupations and industries have a "fair" wage. Ideally, collective bargaining would identify the fair wage for each industry, but since some industries were unable to organize, a minimum wage set by the government was the second-best solution. This philosophy extends the concept of a bargained wage for all workers, not just the most vulnerable.

Fair competition. Early employers in favor of minimum wages argued that competition for factor inputs was unfair, as it would give certain employers an unfair advantage in production costs. A minimum wage could promote fair competition among entrepreneurs.

Macroeconomic objectives. The minimum wage can also be used to affect the entire wage distribution, which may lead to economic growth, inflation control, or political gains, to name a few.

Source: Starr (1993).

By the 1960s, many Latin American countries assigned a larger role to the minimum wage: to be an instrument of macroeconomic policies (Starr 1981). This ambitious role for the minimum wage is particular to LAC. It became a tool for inflation stabilization, economic growth (through increasing purchasing power), poverty reduction, income inequality reduction, and political gains. It took on the role as a numeraire for other social programs, and became so prevalent that workers and employers would specify the value of wages in terms of the "number of minimum wages." Many of these macroeconomic objectives failed, leading to a paring-down of the role of the minimum wage, including legislation to delink wages from the minimum wage and use of alternative macroeconomic tools. However, this has not eliminated use of the minimum wage as a social equity tool, and it still is expected to play a large part in poverty and inequality reduction in the Region.

Minimum wage institution in the English-speaking Caribbean evolved differently. These countries adopted the minimum wage system of their British colonial occupiers, which was the classic implementation of a fair wage system: a series of wage boards that set wages by industry. With independence, several of the countries abandoned the complex wage board system in favor of simpler minimum wages with a poverty reduction objective (Starr 1993).

Theoretical Underpinnings—the Classical Economic View

Economists use the labor market as the starting point for understanding the role of the minimum wage. The most basic view of the impact of the minimum wage begins with a downward-sloping aggregate labor demand curve, capturing the declining marginal return to labor with greater employment. A minimum wage set above market-clearing wage forces firms up the demand curve and reduces employment, either by reducing aggregate output or substitution away from labor to other factors of production.

Such a wage floor is likely to have the impact of reducing the dispersion of wages and guaranteeing a fair or living wage for the poorest workers who retain their jobs. However, moving from the individual to the impact on household income distribution or poverty is less straightforward. Although some workers are now paid more, other workers earning near the minimum will lose their jobs, leaving the net impact on the target population—the poor—dependent on several factors:

The magnitude of the accompanying job loss. A very low elasticity of demand implies that large wage gains can be imposed with little job loss, implying a positive total transfer of income from the firms to the target worker group. In the case of one-company towns where the firm may have monopsony power, there may be no job loss and the minimum simply transfers rents from the firm to the workers. At the other extreme, where the elasticity of demand is high, the loss in income of dismissed workers exceeds that gained by those remaining. An elasticity of 1 implies that there are no net transfers—there is simply redistribution of earnings from the newly unemployed poor to the working poor.

The structure of the social unit. If all families had only one worker, the impact of raising the minimum wage on poverty would not be ambiguous. Those retaining their jobs would gain, and if they were pushed above the poverty line, poverty would decrease. Those dismissed would now be without income and would fall below the poverty line. Often, however, there are multiple workers in a family who pool risks and hence one worker's job loss may be offset by another's wage gain. As the number of working family members increases, the impact on the family approaches that of the working sector as a whole: that is, the net transfer to poor households depends on the elasticity of demand.[3,4]

The overall social insurance context. In most advanced countries, the minimum wage is only one element of an overall social protection system that includes an unemployment benefit that replaces some fraction of dismissed workers' wages. This implies that even in the case of unitary elasticity, there are transfers from the society at large to the poorer groups, generally financed by a progressive tax. Latin America generally lacks systems to support the unemployed.[5] Further, to the degree that the unemployed may include those who are looking for their first job, the usual severance pay system will provide no protection.

The classical view of the minimum wage does not necessarily dovetail with the social justice objectives of the policy. The concept of a "fair" wage is not defined in the model. Instead, the market adjusts to the policy intervention without any consideration of the welfare effects or the social acceptability of the change. Thus, although a higher minimum wage may be socially desirable, the market may not support it. This places policy makers in the difficult role of determining a level of the minimum wage that maximizes social justice objectives while minimizing market distortions. The challenge is even greater in LAC than in the United States or western Europe, given the "two-sector economy" nature of their labor markets.

Two-Sector Economies—Models with a "Covered" and "Uncovered" Sector

The presence of a large informal sector uncovered by labor legislation in LAC alters some predictions of the classical view. In most LAC countries, 30–70 percent of workers are covered (Maloney 2003), so a change in the minimum wage law will not necessarily affect employment of all low-wage earners.

Much of the development literature assumes that the two sectors constitute a dualistic labor market where those who cannot find a job in the formal sector find inferior jobs in the informal sector (Harris and Todaro 1970, Mazumdar 1983, Stiglitz 1984, World Bank 1995, IDB 2000). In this view, a nominal rigidity, such as the minimum wage, that forces the wage in the formal sector above market clearing causes dismissed workers to be absorbed into the informal sector, where wages fall to equate labor supply and demand.

The wage adjustment in the informal sector makes the impact of a rising minimum wage on the distribution of wages ambiguous. Earnings are compressed in the formal sector, but the informal wage relative to the formal wage will fall and informal dispersion may increase as well. In the classical model, where there is no informal sector, these workers would be unemployed and hence a zero wage would enter in dispersion measures. In a dual market, this is no longer the case as they may enter the informal sector.

In fact, the minimum wage may have effects emerging from other channels, for instance, through the increased demand for informal goods from richer formal sector workers. Analytically modeling such general equilibrium impacts becomes quite complex (see, for example, Fiszbein [1992], Agenor and Aizenman [1999], and estimating the final impacts of such nominal rigidities has been attempted by calibrating Computable General Equilibrium models (see May [1993], and Devararjan, Ghanem, and Thierfelder [1997], among others). Such exercises are useful for clarifying the channels of influence and getting plausible orders of magnitude.

Analysis is further complicated by recent literature that argues that the dualistic structure underlying much of this literature, and in particular the assumption of the informal sector as primarily the refuge of those unable to find jobs in the formal sector, describes only a minority of the sector. Rather, the informal sector can be conceived as very heterogeneous, with a large, unregulated entrepreneurial sector where many entrants are, in fact, voluntary and enjoy welfare and even wage gains on leaving formal sector employment (Cunningham and Maloney 2002). Recent work on

Mexico and Argentina (Arango and Malone 2000, Arias 1999) finds that, in fact, most unemployment is generated by the informal sector, and hence it is unlikely that the sector is primarily absorbing formal sector unemployment. Numerous authors (see, for example, Geldstein [2000] argues that entry into formality is not trivial and hence is not be the sector of easy entry for the unemployed.

Numerous Brazilian authors and Maloney and Nuñez (2004) have found a "lighthouse" effect where, in fact, informal salaried workers appear to be *more* affected by the minimum wage than the formal sector. This suggests that the sector is less characterized by being inferior, but rather is able to pick and choose the regulations it complies with. Even though, for a variety of reasons, an informal salaried worker may not receive pension or other benefits, a notion of "fairness" may dictate that his or her wage broadly follows the minimum in the formal sector (Maloney 2003; Maloney and Nuñez 2004; Foguel 1997). This may imply, however, that the effect of minimum wages in LAC, with its formal and informal sectors, is a bit closer to the classical world than originally thought. A rise in the minimum wage may lead to displacing workers in the informal sector to unemployment.

In sum, the impact of a rise in the minimum wage on employment, earnings, the distribution of wages, the distribution of household consumption, and poverty depend on a host of factors that do not allow us to predict, on the basis of theory alone, whether the impact is positive or negative. For this reason, we turn to the empirical evidence.

Empirical Evidence from the OECD Countries

The evidence from the United States and Europe gives a useful starting point for testing these models and the discussion of the effects in Latin America.[6] A wealth of research on the employment and, to a lesser extent, the wage effects of the minimum wage in the United States and western Europe give clear lessons. The studies analyzing the poverty and income inequality effects are much fewer.

An increase in the minimum wage is associated with an increase in wages *for those who earned below or near the new minimum wage*, but these effects are neutralized in the long run. In the United States and the OECD countries, young people constitute the majority of minimum wage earners; thus, teenagers' wages are primarily affected by the minimum wage, with little effect on adult wages. On average, teenagers who were earning above the old minimum wage at the time of the increase experience an immediate increase in wages (Grossman 1983, Neumark, Schweitzer, and Wascher 2000, Katz and Krueger 1992, Card and Krueger 1995, Card, Kramarz, and Lemieux 1999), but a wage decrease in the long run, as the supply of labor increases more than the demand for more skilled workers.

An increase in the minimum wage has little or no impact on employment. Most of the empirical evidence on minimum wage impacts on unemployment in developed countries focuses on teenage workers. For the United States (1970s and 1980s), Canada, Portugal, and Greece, a 10 percent increase in the minimum wage is estimated to decrease teenage employment by 0–3 percent, with higher disemployment elasticities for female than male teenagers (Brown 1999, Ghellab 1998). Conversely, in the United Kingdom (Machin and Manning 1996), the United States (Currie and Fallick 1996; Abowd, Kramarz, and Margoliz 1999; Neumark, Schweitzer, and Wascher 2000), and France (Card, Kramarz, and Lemieux 1999) in the 1990s,[7] employment effects have not been generally identified.

An increase in the minimum wage does not reduce household poverty. The paper written by Neumark and Wascher (1997) is the only one that uses microdata to directly estimate the poverty effects of a change in the minimum wage. They show that an increase in the minimum wage causes an increase in incomes of the poor and near-poor in the United States so that 4.1 percent of rise out of poverty, but 3.9 percent of those who are near-poor fall below the poverty line. The 0.2 percent net decrease in poverty is not statistically significant, indicating no real improvement in aggregate poverty. Instead, the minimum wage redistributes income and jobs among households clustered around the poverty line rather than redistributing income from wealthy households to poor households. Burkhauser, Couch, and Wittenburg (1996) use simulations with similar results, and explain that the absence of any effects is a result of the distribution of minimum wage earners across the population, rather than being concentrated in low-income households.

The minimum wage effects on family income inequality are mixed. In the United States, an increase in wage inequality from 1973 to 1992 is attributed to a fall in the real value of the minimum wage, especially among women (DiNardo, Fortin, and Lemieux 1996), but no effects on family income inequality were observed (Horrigan and Mincy 1993). Card and Krueger (1995) find that a 26.6 percent increase in the minimum wage leads to an increase in family income by an average of 6 percent for families in the lowest wealth decile and an increase in family income of 2.5 percent for families in the fifth (median) decile, whereas no changes in family income are detected in the top wealth deciles. However, the results are not strongly statistically identified.

Minimum wage effects differ little by gender and race. In the United States, the minimum wage does not have a larger effect on the wages or employment of women, as compared to men, or of black workers as compared to white workers (Brown 1999). An exception is DiNardo, Fortin, and Lemieux (1996), who find that a higher minimum wage increases female within-gender inequality, but this is not true of men.

The Latin American Research

If the preceding findings, mixed as they are, could be applied to Latin America, policy makers would have good information with which to develop minimum wage policies. However, there are various reasons to expect that the OECD findings will not tell the whole LAC story. First, LAC has a very large informal sector. As discussed earlier in this chapter, minimum wage effects in a dualistic economy are difficult to predict. Since 30–70 percent of LAC's workers are employed in the informal sector, this is a significant issue, requiring empirical work to sort out the effects. Unfortunately, the evidence of minimum wage impacts on informal sector workers in the United States and western Europe is very scarce, largely because their informal sectors are very small.

Second, the low-wage population in LAC includes adults. Most of the minimum wage effects in the OECD were identified among youth, since they are the population group clustered around the minimum wage. In LAC, though, adults are also low-wage earners. Thus, the conclusion by Burkhauser, Couch, and Wittenburg (1996) that minimum wages have little effect on household poverty since they largely affect secondary household workers, is less applicable to LAC, where minimum wage policies may affect the primary income earner in the household.

Third, the minimum wage acts as a numerator in LAC. During periods of hyperinflation, wages were indexed to inflation in several Latin American countries, so the minimum became a standard against which to measure wages. Although such indexing does not formally exist in LAC at the present, the informal practice of denominating wages in terms of the value of the minimum wage still does.

Fourth, LAC has weak social protection systems. The Region has gone through an extensive overhaul of its labor market since its rapid entry into the world market in the 1980s. The social protection systems that were effective under closed economies are no longer suitable. Thus, countries are in the process of redesigning their social protection models to create integrated, cohesive, and comprehensive systems. These complementary programs are crucial for changing incentives and thus how minimum wages will affect wages, employment, household poverty, and income inequality.

Although research on minimum wages in Latin America is relatively new, there is a body of work, mostly for Brazil, examining the employment and wage impacts of minimum wages.[8] These papers will be reviewed in detail throughout this report (and summarized in appendix II), but in general, they show that minimum wages have different effects in Latin America from those in the United States and Europe: The minimum wage has strong effects on employment and wages, the effects are felt throughout the wage distribution, and the minimum wage plays a role in the informal sector.

These findings will be further tested in this report and the question of the minimum wage effects on poverty, inequality, special groups, and the public finances will also be addressed.

Notes

1. The concept of the "maximum wage" first emerged in medieval Europe. The Black Death killed between one-third to one-half of the population in the 14th century, leading to a severe labor shortage and increasing the price of labor. In England, the landowners who depended on this labor were also the policy makers. They passed acts defining a maximum wage: workers and employers could bargain on the amount of time worked, but the payment was capped. Violations of the law were punishable by a fine equal to six months of the maximum wage. The severe shortage of labor led to secret informal arrangements among skilled laborers and their employers; these skilled laborers eventually banded together in trade unions and the famous "secret societies," including the Freemasons (Ridley 1999).

2. Mexico was the first country in the world to include in the constitution a guarantee for minimum wages. Argentina (1918), Costa Rica (1934), Brazil (1938), Ecuador (1896—transport of kerosene and 1900—agricultural sector), Uruguay (1923—agricultural sector), and Peru (1916—indigenous peoples, 1922—maritime workers, 1937—home workers) were also early leaders in implementing some limited occupation-specific version of a minimum wage (Starr 1993).

3. Various models of household dynamics suggest that income is not shared equally among household members. Unlike the Mincer (1962) and Becker

(1976) models, where the household head (the person with the most power in the household) is altruistic and ensures an equitable distribution of household resources, these alternative models assume a cooperative or even an uncooperative bargaining game where the outcome is not necessarily Pareto Optimal. In other words, the person who has the most power in the household and makes resource allocation decisions will not necessarily distribute household income in such a way that everyone is equally well off. See Haddad, Hoddinott, and Alderman (1997) for a review of household bargaining models.

4. The minimum wage may also contribute to noneconomic well-being. For example, if an increase in the minimum wage leads to higher earnings of women, they may have more say in how household resources are spent or on the formation and dissolution of the household. The intrahousehold dynamics of minimum wages are not covered in this paper.

5. Notable exceptions include Brazil, Argentina, Uruguay, and Chile.

6. For a full exposition of the OECD literature, see Brown (1999).

7. More recent studies in the United States and France, using longer time series and more careful analysis, find mixed results, but maintain that the employment effects are small to nil.

8. No minimum wage research using data from the Caribbean was identified during the preparation of this study.

CHAPTER 3

Minimum Wage Institutions in LAC: What Are They and Who Earns Them?

What Is a Minimum Wage?

In the simplest terms, a minimum wage is a legally mandated lower bound for wages, but the term "legally mandated" is vague, leading to many different kinds of minimum wage institutions. In the most straightforward cases, such as Brazil or Bolivia, the federal government identifies a wage level and all employers in the country must pay at that level or above it. In other countries, such as the United States, a federal minimum wage may be increased by a state-specific minimum wage. Yet other countries, such as Italy, have a collection of wages that are negotiated by trade unions, thus blurring the distinction between a minimum wage and a contract wage. In such cases, the question may be asked whether Italy has a minimum wage at all, or whether it simply has many negotiated wages that are backed by an effective monitoring network and an able judicial system (Trinder 1984).

The coverage, enforcement, and degree to which the minimum wage affects the wage distribution differ across countries. The *coverage* of the minimum wage is that fraction of the population for whom the policy is legally guaranteed—that is, the formal sector. A minimum wage is *enforced* if everyone who is covered earns at least the minimum. Finally, it is *binding* if it actually affects wage distribution, whether through enforcement or other factors. It is *completely binding* if it creates a wage floor, whereas it is

19

somewhat binding if it creates a distortion of the wage distribution, which may not be a wage floor. This report finds that in LAC, minimum wages cover 30–70 percent of the population (that is, the formal sector), and although they are generally not enforced, they are somewhat binding.

There Is No Common "Minimum Wage System" for LAC

All LAC countries have a legislated minimum wage system. The common goal of the systems is to set a wage floor that provides a minimum standard of living for the worker and, in some cases, his or her family. Minimum wages are usually constitutionally mandated, in some cases dating back to the 1930s, when the concept of a minimum wage was new to the world. The individual institutions that have developed in LAC over time cover a wide range of minimum wage levels, categories, and wage-setting mechanisms (see table 3.1).

Minimum wage systems vary widely across the Region. Whereas Argentina, the Bahamas, Bolivia, Brazil, Haiti, and Trinidad and Tobago are the only countries in LAC with a single minimum wage, and many others have a few well- defined minimum wages (two in Colombia and Jamaica, three in Chile, and four in Belize and Peru), some countries, such as the Dominican Republic, Ecuador, Guatemala, Mexico, Paraguay, and the República Bolivariana de Venezuela have hundreds of legislated minimum wages. Special minimum wages may be set for apprentices (Colombia, Chile, El Salvador, Guatemala, Honduras, Paraguay, Trinidad and Tobago, and the República Bolivariana de Venezuela); the public sector (Argentina, Brazil, Chile, Costa Rica, the Dominican Republic, Ecuador, Honduras, Jamaica, Panama, and Peru); youth (Argentina, Belize, Chile, Costa Rica, Paraguay, Trinidad and Tobago, and the República Bolivariana de Venezuela); part-time workers (Mexico); domestic workers (Haiti, Nicaragua, Paraguay, and Uruguay); or specific occupations (see box 3.1). All countries define a minimum wage by time spent working (hour, day, or month), but some have extra legislation by task (Uruguay, the Dominican Republic), or output quantity (the Dominican Republic, Guatemala, and Jamaica). The coverage of the minimum wage may be national (Brazil, Colombia, Chile), regional (Mexico), by occupation or industry or activity (Ecuador), task, firm size, or any mix of these (table 3.1).

Tripartite wage setting is associated with complex minimum wage systems. Although the government alone sets the minimum wage in some countries (Brazil, Bolivia, Ecuador, Jamaica, Uruguay), a tripartite committee composed of government, worker representatives, and employer

Table 3.1. Main Institutional Characteristics Affecting Minimum Wages in Selected Latin American Countries

Country	Number of minimum wages	Work period covered by the mw (monthly (M), weekly (W), daily (D), hourly (H), by task (T), by output (O))	Scope of mw setting (national (N), regional (R), sector (S), occupation (O), task (T), firm size (W))	Body that sets the mw (government (G) or tripartite (T), in order of dominance)	Frequency changed	Criteria for adjustment (inflation (I), needs of worker & family (N), cost of living (L), economic development, (D), labor market conditions (M), firm capacity to pay (C), equity (E), other/unclear/political (O))	Sub-minimum payments	Mw applied to public sector (yes, no, or own rate)	Sanctions for non-compliance	Notes
Argentina	1	M, H	N (S, O)	T	discretion	N, E	workfare programs, disabled workers, trainees, youth	own	$250 to $1,000 per worker	d, h

(continued)

Table 3.1. Main Institutional Characteristics Affecting Minimum Wages in Selected Latin American Countries (continued)

Country	Number of minimum wages	Work period covered by the mw	Scope of mw setting	Body that sets the mw	Frequency changed	Criteria for adjustment	Sub-minimum payments	Mw applied to public sector	Sanctions for non-compliance	Notes
Bolivia	1	M	N	G	annual	I, N, D	no	yes	n.a.	C, i
Brazil	1	M	N	G	annual	I	no	own	$170 per worker	
Bahamas	1	W, H	N	G, T	discretion	O	no	yes	n.a.	
Haiti	1	D	N	G, T	discretion	L, I	domestic workers	yes	n.a.	
Trinidad and Tobago	1	H, D, W, M	N	T, G	discretion	L, M, D, C	trainees, apprentices, workfare, students, volunteers	yes	n.a.	
Colombia	2	D	N	T, G	annual	L, M, C, I, G	apprentice	yes	1 to 100 x mw	
Jamaica	2	W, H	N, O	G	1–3 years	I, N	casual labor	own	none	
Chile	3	M	N	G, T	annual	I. L, M, O	under 18, apprentices, over 65, mentally disabled workers	own	fines by firm size	f
Belize	4	H	I	T, G	discretion	O	students	yes	n.a.	

									fines by firm size [g]	
Peru	4	M	N	T, G	discretion	N, D	no	no		
Cuba	6	n.a.	O, S	G, T	n.a.	D, E	no	yes	n.a.	
El Salvador	8	D	S, T	G, T	3 years	N, L, D, O	apprentices	yes	n.a.	
Honduras	12	D	S, W	T, G	6 months	P, L, G, C, I	apprentices, disabled workers	no	$30 to $300	[b]
Nicaragua	12	M, D	S	T	6 months–1 year	N, D	domestic workers	yes	25% mw	
Uruguay	21	M, D, T	N, R, S, O	G	annual	N, D, C, I, O	domestic or rural workers	no	1 to 150 mw per worker	
Costa Rica	25	H, D, M	S, O	T	6 months	I, L, D	youth	own	1 to 23 mw	[e]
Panama	30	H	R, S, W	G, T	2 years	L, D, C, O	no	no	$25 to $150	
Mexico	91	D	R, O	T	yearly/ discretion	N, D, C, I, L, M	part-time workers	yes	none under federal law	
Dom. Rep	~271 (by sector)	M, D, T, H, O	S, O, T	T	discretion	N, L, M, C	no	own	3 to 6 mw	[f]
Ecuador	~150 (by sector)	M	S, O	G	6 months	I	no	own	2 to 5 mw	
Guatemala	hundreds (by sector)	D, O	S, I	T, G	annual	L, N, M, C	apprentices	own	fines/prison	

(continued)

Table 3.1. Main Institutional Characteristics Affecting Minimum Wages in Selected Latin American Countries (continued)

Country	Number of minimum wages	Work period covered by the mw	Scope of mw setting	Body that sets the mw	Frequency changed	Criteria for adjustment	Sub-minimum payments	Mw applied to public sector	Sanctions for non-compliance	Notes
Paraguay	hundreds (by sector)	M, D	N, O, S	T, G	discretion	N, L, M, C, O	apprentices, youth, disabled workers, domestic workers	no	10 to 30 mw	a
Venezuela, R.B. de	hundreds (by sector)	M	R, S, I, O	T, G	annual	P, G, L	apprentices, youth	yes	n.a	a

Source: Interviews with labor ministries; Gonzaga and Scandiuzzi (1998); Ruiz (2001); Starr (1993); www1.umn.edu/humanrts/esc/bolivia2001.html; www.salaryexpert.com/seco/careerjournal/hrcodes/COUNTRIES.htm; www.ilo.org/public/english/dialogue/govlab/legrel/papers/brfnotes/minwages; www.mintrab.cl; www.mtps.gob.pe; www.stps.gov.mx; www.set.gov.do/legislacion/salariomin/index.htm; www.ilo.org/travaildatabase/servlet/minimumwages; www.dol.gov/ILAB/media/reports/oiea/wagestudy.

n.a. data are not available. mw = minimum wage. ~ = about.

a. Automatic adjustment if the inflation rate rises by 10 percent or more.

b. Fines are rarely imposed, only large firms are generally inspected.

c. Incomplete information since the department of labor inspection is located outside ministry and without telephones.

d. Enforcement generally at regional level—no information currently available.

e. The ministry does not impose fines; it only warns and takes to court.

f. Codigo del trabajo Art. 44 & Art. 477: firms with 1 to 49 workers: $40 to $800 monthly per worker affected. Firms with 50 to 199 workers: $80 to $1,600 monthly per worker affected. Firms with more than 200 workers: $120 to $2,400 monthly per worker affected.

g. The fines are a function of the number of workers and the number of infractions. Fines range from the equivalent of US$200 for first infraction with 1–5 workers to US$1,800 for multiple infractions involving hundreds of workers.

h. Legally, 1,500 minimum wages are on the books, as a result of the bargaining under the military dictatorship. In practice, though, only one minimum wage applies.

i. According to Article 121 of the Supreme Decree 21615 (29 May, 1987), the labor judges may impose a fine of $1,000–10,000 *bolivianos* for infractions.

representatives is the wage-setting body in others (Argentina, Bolivia, Colombia, Costa Rica, the Dominican Republic, Guatemala, Honduras, Mexico, Nicaragua, Peru, Paraguay, Trinidad and Tobago, and the República Bolivariana de Venezuela).[1] In several countries (the Bahamas, Chile, Cuba, El Salvador, Haiti, and Panama), the minimum wage is recommended by nongovernmental groups or tripartite committees, but the final level is set by the national government. Those countries with the most complex wage structure—hundreds of minimum wages—tend to be those where the wage is set by a tripartite council.[2]

The minimum wage is changed every six months or one year in about half the countries, with discretionary changes in others (Argentina, the Bahamas, Belize, the Dominican Republic, Haiti, Paraguay, Peru, and Trinidad and Tobago). Adjustments to the minimum wage may be tied to inflation (in half the countries), GDP fluctuations, the poverty line, or market wages (table 3.1). In Paraguay and Haiti, the legislation states that inflation rates equal to or higher than 10 percent should trigger renegotiation of the minimum wage.

Sanctions for noncompliance are regulated in many, but not all, countries. The fines imposed on firms that do not abide by minimum wage laws range from one to 150 times the minimum wage (table 3.1). No

---

Box 3.1

Protecting the Wages of Soccer Players

Occupation-specific minimum wages are widespread in Latin America, particularly in those countries where occupational or industry groups bargain the minimum. Although wages are set for typical low-paying occupations, others are assigned to very specific, not necessarily low-paying, occupations or to those that are difficult to enforce. For example:

- Peruvian soccer players, miners, and journalists have their own minimum wage.
- A wage floor for the self-employed is legislated in Chile.
- Street vendors—*pica pollos or chimichurras*—each have their own minimum wage in the Dominican Republic.
- Workers on bee or rabbit farms are specially protected in Mexico.
- Guatemalan bakers and pastry workers who are not paid daily are awarded a premium above the minimum wage.

Source: Minimum wage legislation for each country.

fines or punishments are legislated in Jamaica, Costa Rica, or Mexico. In some countries, enforcement is legislated but not carried out because of a lack of resources—ranging from no vehicles for the inspectors to conduct inspections, to no telephones to receive complaints from workers. The scarce data on enforcement show that fines are rarely imposed. In Chile, for example, 244 fines were issued in 2001, totaling $60,000, as compared to the $2.9 million collected in fines for all labor violations that year.

Who Earns the Minimum Wage?

Up to 20 percent of the labor force in LAC countries earns the minimum wage. Figure 3.1 shows the proportion of the labor force that earns below, equal to, and above the minimum wage in each of 19 countries, using the most recent year for which data could be obtained (appendix III describes the data).[3] More than 10 percent of the labor force earns the minimum wage in Brazil, Ecuador, Panama, and the República Bolivariana de Venezuela, whereas less than 5 percent are minimum wage earners in 12 other countries. The lowest proportion is in Uruguay, with 0.5 percent of the population; the highest proportion

Figure 3.1. Distribution of Minimum Wage Earners

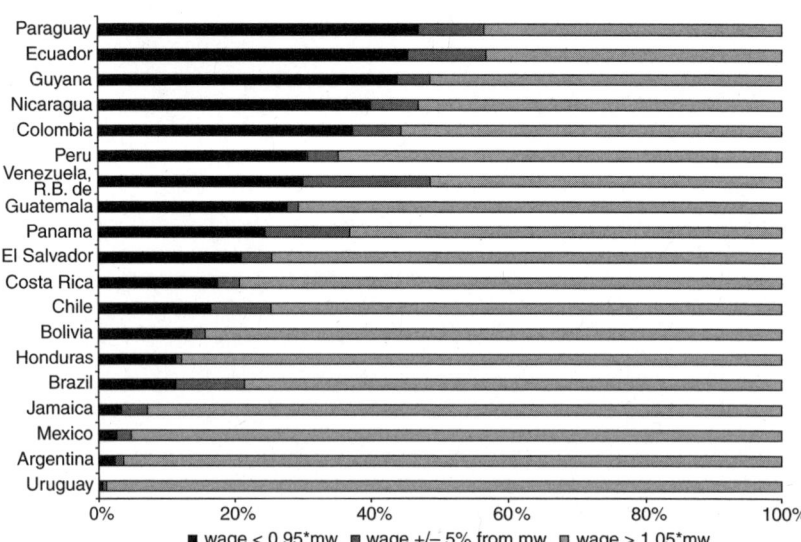

Source: Kristensen and Cunningham (2006).
Note: Although several of these countries have hundreds of minimum wages (table 3.1), the most frequently repeated level or (if this was not evident) the average minimum wage was used for this exercise.

is in the República Bolivariana de Venezuela and Panama, with 20 and 13 percent, respectively.[4] A low proportion of minimum wage earners does not indicate that the minimum wage is unimportant: as will be shown in this report, it may have effects throughout the wage distribution. Or it may be important for certain subgroups of the population, such as young workers, as is the case in the United States and Europe.

The minimum wage is not strictly binding in LAC. Figure 3.1 shows that there are subminimum workers in all countries. The size of the subminimum population is larger than the minimum wage population in all countries, ranging from 0.7 to 45 percent of the workforce. More than 40 percent of the workforce of Nicaragua, Guyana, Ecuador, and Paraguay are subminimum workers, whereas less than 3 percent earn below the minimum in Mexico, Argentina, and Uruguay.

Young, informal, and less educated workers are overrepresented among the minimum wage population. Similar to the OECD countries, young workers are overrepresented among minimum and subminimum wage earners. The first column of table 3.2 shows the ratios of 16- to 19-year-olds who are minimum wage earners (relative to the whole minimum wage population) to the ratio of the working population age 16–19 (relative to the whole working population). A value greater than 1.0 indicates that the young are a larger share of the minimum wage earners than they are of the labor force as a whole. The table shows that in all but four countries in the sample, those who are age 16–19 are a larger share of the minimum wage population than the general population. Of the countries in the sample, the young are the most overrepresented among minimum wage earners in Uruguay (ratio = 2.6), whereas they are the least overrepresented in Paraguay (ratio = 0.3) and Ecuador (ratio = 0.4). Young workers are even more overrepresented among the subminimum population (first column of table 3.3).

Employees in the informal sector are overrepresented among minimum and subminimum wage workers. In all countries except Honduras, Panama, and Paraguay, the ratio in table 3.2 is greater than 1, with particularly high ratios in Mexico (3.7), Guatemala (2.0), Chile (1.9), and Brazil (1.8). These trends are reflected in the subminimum population. Although it may be argued that this is spurious correlation, as informal sector employees tend to be low-skilled and their marginal productivity therefore may happen to coincide with the minimum wage, later sections of this report show that this is not necessarily the case.

The less skilled are more represented in the minimum wage sector in most of the Region. With the exception of Costa Rica, Ecuador, Panama,

Table 3.2. Ratio of Each Subgroup's Share of the Minimum Wage Population, Relative to Its Share of the Total Workforce (Full-Time Workers Only)

0.95 < w/mw < 1.05	16–19 years	55–64 years	No school	Primary school	Informal employee	Self-employed	Female
Argentina	n.a.	n.a.	n.a.	2.0	n.a.	n.a.	1.3
Bolivia	1.6	3.0	2.1	1.9	1.0	1.5	1.0
Brazil	2.1	0.9	1.4	1.2	1.8	0.5	1.4
Chile	1.7	0.7	1.7	1.5	1.9	n.a.	1.1
Colombia	1.0	0.7	1.2	1.2	1.4	0.7	1.0
Costa Rica	1.5	1.2	0.6	1.5	n.a.	n.a.	1.0
Ecuador	0.4	0.8	0.7	1.1	0.9	0.9	0.9
El Salvador	1.4	0.3	1.4	1.6	1.0	n.a.	1.1
Guatemala	1.5	1.2	1.1	0.9	2.0	0.7	1.0
Guyana	1.1	1.1	1.7	0.8	n.a.	0.4	1.1
Honduras	0.3	n.a.	1.4	n.a.	0.4	n.a.	1.3
Jamaica	1.8	1.9	6.5	1.6	1.5	3.0	1.2
Mexico	1.9	1.6	3.4	1.3	3.7	1.7	1.3
Nicaragua	1.1	1.1	1.2	0.9	n.a.	n.a.	1.1
Panama	1.3	0.7	0.9	1.3	0.9	0.9	1.0
Paraguay	0.3	0.8	0.3	0.9	0.9	n.a.	0.8
Peru	1.2	0.4	0.2	1.0	1.2	0.4	0.8
Uruguay	2.6	1.0	1.7	1.4	n.a.	n.a.	1.3
Venezuela, R.B. de	1.2	0.8	0.8	1.1	1.2	0.7	1.1

Source: Kristensen and Cunningham (2006).
Note: Omitted categories are, respectively, age 20–54, male, formal employee, and secondary school or above.
n.a. data were not available to generate the statistic.
A value greater than 1 indicates that the reference group is overrepresented among the minimum wage population.

Paraguay, Peru, and the República Bolivariana de Venezuela, those without any formal education are a larger share of the minimum wage population than the general working population. This trend is even stronger for the subminimum population, where they are overrepresented in all countries. The trends for primary education are similar (tables 3.2 and 3.3).

Women, older workers, and the self-employed are neither more nor less likely to be minimum wage workers. Table 3.2 shows that throughout the Region, women's share of the minimum wage population is similar to their share of the working population (near the value of 1). The exceptions are Argentina, Brazil, Honduras, Mexico, and Uruguay, where the ratio is a value of 1.3 or higher. Similarly, women are not necessarily overrepresented among the subminimum population, although certain outliers emerge, namely Bolivia, Honduras, Mexico, and Uruguay. However, the countries where women are overrepresented among minimum wage workers are not

Table 3.3. Ratio of Each Subgroup's Share of the Subminimum Wage Population, Relative to Its Share of the Total Workforce (Full-Time Workers Only)

0.95 > w/mw	16–19 years	55–64 years	No school	Primary sector	Informal sector	Self-employed	Female
Argentina	n.a.	n.a.	8.1	1.7	n.a.	n.a.	1.0
Bolivia	1.9	1.6	2.6	1.3	0.8	1.9	1.8
Brazil	2.2	1.6	3.3	1.2	2.3	1.8	1.0
Chile	2.9	0.7	1.8	1.5	2.4	n.a.	1.1
Colombia	1.8	0.9	1.6	1.1	1.3	1.4	1.0
Costa Rica	2.3	1.3	3.1	1.8	0.2	n.a.	1.3
Ecuador	1.9	1.0	1.8	1.5	1.0	1.1	1.1
El Salvador	2.5	1.8	3.0	1.4	1.0	n.a.	1.0
Guatemala	1.7	2.8	2.1	1.2	1.2	2.0	1.1
Guyana	1.8	0.8	1.4	1.1	n.a.	1.0	1.3
Honduras	1.9	1.3.	1.1	n.a.	1.5	n.a.	1.5
Jamaica	1.5	1.3	n.a.	1.4	1.0	3.8	1.1
Mexico	2.0	2.0	4.7	1.4	3.4	2.4	1.8
Nicaragua	1.6	0.9	1.4	1.3	n.a.	n.a.	1.1
Panama	2.8	1.1	2.4	1.7	1.7	1.3	0.7
Paraguay	1.9	0.8	1.9	1.6	1.5	n.a.	1.1
Peru	2.4	0.9	2.6	1.4	2.0	1.1	1.2
Uruguay	5.0	0.8	3.4	1.5	n.a.	n.a.	1.5
Venezuela, R.B. de	1.9	1.2	2.1	1.2	1.7	1.4	1.2

Source: Kristensen and Cunningham (2006).
Note: Omitted categories are, respectively, age 20–54, male, formal employee, and secondary school and above.
n.a. the data are not available to calculate the statistic.
A value greater than 1 indicates that the reference group is overrepresented among the subminimum wage population.

necessarily those where they are overrepresented among subminimum wage workers. A note of caution is necessary, however, since the table considers only full-time workers; expanding the sample to include part-time employees, among which women are overrepresented, may lead to a different conclusion.

Across the Region, older workers (age 55–64 years old) are not uniformly over- or underrepresented among minimum wage earners. Although age-earning profiles tend to show that real wages for workers begin to decline around age 50, they do not necessarily revert to the minimum wage. Older workers are a lower share of the minimum wage population than the entire working population in countries as diverse as Brazil, Chile, Colombia, Ecuador, Panama, Paraguay, Peru, and the República Bolivariana de Venezuela. Conversely, in the equally diverse countries of Bolivia, Costa Rica, Guatemala, Jamaica, Mexico, and

Nicaragua, workers age 55–64 are a higher share of the minimum wage population than the general population.

The self-employed are largely underrepresented among minimum wage earners. In the small sample where the self-employed could be identified, they were overrepresented among the minimum wage earners only in Bolivia, Jamaica, and Mexico, with ratios between 0.14 and 0.9 for the other eight countries in the sample. Alternatively, the self-employed are overrepresented among the subminimum population in all countries in the sample. This may suggest a greater relative number of workers with very low incomes in the self-employment sector, with a thinning of the population near the minimum wage. Or it may suggest a smooth distribution for the self-employed whose incomes we would not expect to be affected by the minimum wage, as opposed to a "sweeping up" of low-income employees whose incomes are near the mandated minimum.

Groups that are overrepresented among minimum wage earners may still have low proportions who actually earn at or below the minimum wage. Although tables 3.2 and 3.3 show how over- or underrepresented various demographic groups are relative to their share of the labor force, they do not reveal what proportion of that group earns the minimum wage. Table 3.4 shows the proportion of workers within each demographic group who earn at or below the minimum wage, which suggests that even if individuals are overrepresented among the minimum wage population, they may not be overwhelmingly minimum wage workers. For example, young workers are overrepresented among minimum wage workers in Mexico, but only 25.6 percent of the young earn the minimum wage. A similar situation prevails for informal sector workers, where less than 30 percent of them earn less than the minimum wage.

Table 3.4. Proportion that Earns at or below the Minimum Wage, by Demographic Characteristic

	Argentina (1999)	Brazil (1996–2000)	Colombia (1984–2001)	Mexico (1999)
Young (age < 19)	70.0	40.0	63.0	25.6
Female	19.9	21.8	25.7	13.2
Informal sector	31.7	23.0	n.a.	16.9
Primary school or less	24.6	26.0	55.0	11.9
Household wealth quintile 1	24.5	n.a.	75.0	14.6
Household wealth quintile 5	5.6	n.a.	7.7	4.1

Source: Argentina and Mexico (Cunningham 2002), Brazil (Neumark, Cunningham, and Siga 2003), Colombia (Arango and Pachon 2003).
n.a. the value was not reported.

Wages of workers whose marginal productivity is near the minimum wage may converge to the minimum wage. Uruguay, Jamaica, Brazil, Argentina, Mexico, and Bolivia have the lowest ratio of minimum wage workers and also have more women, low-educated, and youth at the minimum than expected. Thus, even though the minimum wage population is small in these countries, it disproportionately affects certain population groups—the groups that are often the hardest to employ, whether because of time constraints (school, family care) that limit job choice, frequent entry into and exit from the labor market, or lower human capital because of less job experience or lower education levels. Conversely, in countries where a high share of the population consists of minimum or subminimum wage earners—namely Paraguay and Ecuador—women, unskilled, and the young are *under*represented among minimum wage earners. Thus, given the distribution of productivity and corresponding wages, the minimum wage may have the effect of sweeping up those whose productivity (and market wage) are near the minimum, but may not affect the wages of those whose market wage is far from the mandated minimum.

How High Is the Minimum Wage in LAC

Minimum wage levels vary widely across Latin America. Table 3.5 shows the level of the minimum wage for 20 countries in the Region, in national currency and in PPP-adjusted U.S. dollars. The minimum wage is the most generous in Paraguay, at more than US$500 monthly (PPP-adjusted), and the least generous in Uruguay, at PPP-adjusted US$45 monthly. Although Paraguay has the highest proportion of individuals at or below the minimum and Uruguay the lowest, the absence of correlation between these two factors for the other 18 countries in the sample suggests that the proportion of minimum wage earners is largely independent of the PPP-adjusted level of the minimum wage.

The minimum wage is far below the mean wage in all countries in the Region, but this does not imply that the minimum wage is not well set. Figure 3.2 shows that the ratio of minimum to mean wages ranges from 18 percent of the mean wage (Uruguay) to 72 percent of the mean wage (Paraguay). Half of the sample countries have ratios between 20 and 40 percent of the respective mean wages. Three of the four countries with the highest ratio also have the largest share of their population earning the minimum wage; Brazil is the outlier, with a large share earning the minimum but a low wage ratio. Similarly, the country ranking of the

Table 3.5. Minimum Wages in LAC

Country	Year	Monthly mw, domestic currency	Mw in PPP-adjusted US$
Paraguay	2000	680168	$546
El Salvador	1998	1,083	$446
Dominican Republic	1997	2,412	$429
Costa Rica	1999	54,938	$423
Chile	2001	100,000	$335
Colombia	1999	236,438	$293
Guatemala	2000	712	$289
Honduras	1999	1419	$221
Brazil	1999	136	$205
Argentina	2000	200	$200
Panama	1998	206	$185
Guyana	1999	19,000	$181
Peru	1999	345	$124
Bolivia	1999	330	$90
Jamaica	1998	800	$75
Ecuador	1998	762,967	$75
Venezuela, R.B. de	1998	100,000	$54
Mexico	1999	888.81	$50
Uruguay	1998	990	$45
Nicaragua	2001	1,000	n.a.

Source: Kristensen and Cunningham (2006).
n.a. no data were available.

share of the population earning below the minimum wage (figure 3.1) is similar to the country ranking of the minimum wage to mean wage ratio (figure 3.2)—that is, countries with higher relative minimum wages are also those with more people earning less than the minimum.

Perhaps a more appropriate relative measure is the median wage, as it omits very high earners. Maloney and Nuñez (2004) find that the ratio of the minimum wage to the median wage ranges from 27 percent (in Uruguay) to 69 percent (in Colombia) (table 3.6), compared to the ratio of the minimum wage to the mean wage, which is 18 percent and 52 percent, respectively.

The minimum wage is similar to the average wage of unskilled workers in most countries. To control for the skill differentials in the comparison of minimum wages to market wages, a better comparator group may be "unskilled workers," who have productivity levels more similar to workers at the bottom of the wage distribution. The ratio of minimum wages to mean wages of the unskilled ranges from 0.21 to 1.4, indicating

Figure 3.2. Minimum Wage Relative to the Mean or Unskilled Wage

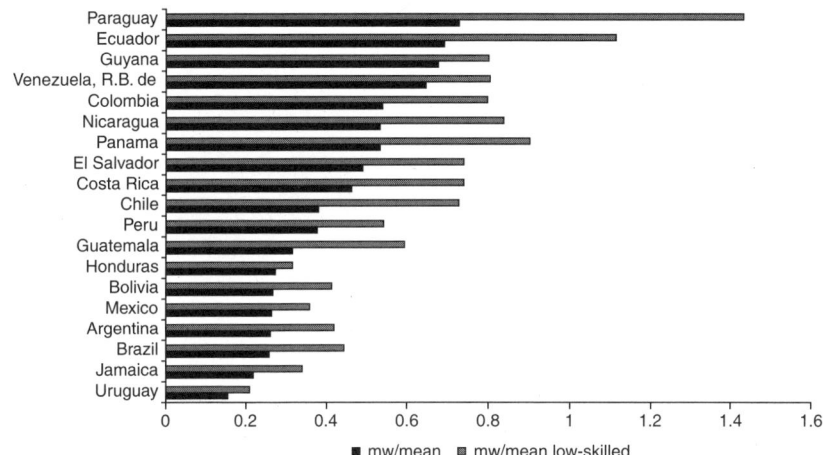

Source: Kristensen and Cunningham (2006).

Table 3.6. Ratio of the Minimum Wage to the Median and 10th Percentile Wages, %

	Mw/median	Mw/10th percentile
Argentina	33	67
Brazil	43	100
Bolivia	34	80
Chile	55	109
Colombia	68	100
Mexico	48	87
Uruguay	27	64

Source: Maloney and Nuñez (2004).

that the minimum wage is 40 percent higher than the average wage of unskilled workers in Paraguay and 89 percent below the similar comparator group in Uruguay (figure 3.2). Ten of the 18 sample countries show that minimum wages are greater than 70 percent of the average unskilled wage. A similar exercise by Maloney and Nuñez (2004) uses the 10th percentile wage as the base (table 3.6); they show an even higher correlation between the minimum-wage and low-wage workers.

A standard established by the Brazilian Institute for Applied Economics (Instituto de Pesquisa Economica Aplicada, IPEA) is that the international norm is a minimum wage that is at least 40 percent of the average manufacturing wage. This conclusion was reached by examining the minimum wage to manufacturing wage ratio in countries across the world and observing a clustering at 40 percent (IPEA 2002). The conclusion is complicated by the fact that the productivity of manufacturing workers is likely to be much higher than that of unskilled workers in other sectors. Thus, the conclusion may be the result of productivity differences between the manufacturing and low-skilled workers and is therefore determined by the market. If, indeed, low-skilled workers are more than 60 percent less productive than the manufacturing sector, then this 40 percent may reflect a global sense of fairness. However, it would be useful to identify a comparator group in which the skill level is similar between the types of workers who earn the minimum wage and the comparator group, as shown above.

Notes

1. In Colombia, for example, workers and employer representatives select the minimum wage. If they cannot agree on a wage, the government sets the wage.

2. If unions and employers define the minimum wage, it is preferred to have multiple minimum wages so that the agreed-on union wage is not imposed on the whole country in the form of a single minimum wage, which may be too high for nonunion employment.

3. A wage is considered "equal to" the minimum wage in this exercise if it is within 5 percent of the minimum wage. A range rather than a single value of the minimum wage is used to compensate for measurement errors in the data: wages are reported in the surveys as monthly wages, but minimum wages are often reported hourly, daily, or weekly. Thus, aggregating the "minimum wage" to a monthly comparison requires assumptions about the hours worked per day and days worked per week.

4. Since the minimum wage is a "round number," equal to 100,000 in Chile and the República Bolivariana de Venezuela, the apparent exact payment of the minimum may actually be due to a convention to pay round numbers or due to reporting bias that rounds the wage.

CHAPTER 4

The Worker: How Do Minimum Wages Affect Other Wages and Employment?

The usefulness of the minimum wage as a social protection tool depends not only on its ability to redistribute income, but also on how well it does this compared to alternative tools. Ultimately, we are interested in how the minimum wage affects poverty and inequality, but this section focuses on the worker to give us the building blocks for the next chapter, which considers the household. It allows us to identify who is distributing income to whom, and whether this meets the government's and society's objectives.

Minimum Wages Are Somewhat Binding

An examination of wage distributions can give us some insight into whether or not the minimum wage is enforced and binding. If workers are paid a wage equal to their marginal productivity, and if the latter is continuously distributed across the population, we would expect a smooth wage distribution. However, if there is an exogenous factor such as a minimum wage that affects wage setting, the distribution will not be smooth. Instead, we will see a "spike" in the distribution. To be sure that our "spikes" are not statistical artifacts, we also plot the number of people earning up to a specific wage (cumulative density plot) and examine whether a "cliff" is visible at the wage corresponding to the minimum wage. If the wage level at the spike and at the cliff for a particular country coincides with the value of the minimum, we can then assume that the minimum wage is to blame for the discontinuity in the wage distribution: it is *binding*.[1] If everyone earns above the minimum and it is binding, this suggests that the minimum is *enforced*.

The minimum wage is not enforced in Latin America. In all countries in the Region, there are individuals *in both the formal and informal sectors who earn below the minimum wage*.[2] Appendix IV plots the wages of formal and informal sector workers and indicates where the minimum wage falls in each distribution (the vertical line). Very few individuals are subminimum earners in Argentina, Jamaica, Mexico, and Uruguay, which are also the countries with the lowest PPP-adjusted minimum wage. Although this may suggest that the minimum is well enforced in those countries, the absence of a "spike" at the vertical line (left graph in each row of appendix IV), which would graphically show that those who would be subminimum workers are pulled up to the minimum wage, suggests that it does not serve as a wage floor. Furthermore, it is unlikely to shift the whole distribution to the right, as the low ratio of minimum to unskilled wages shown in figure 3.2 suggests that the minimum wage is below market wages in these countries, and not that it successfully creates a wage floor. This is supported by the information presented in table 3.1, in which low sanctions or inefficient monitoring systems suggest that enforcement is very low.

The minimum wage is somewhat binding, particularly among those in the informal sector. If skills were continuously distributed across the labor force and institutions that affect the wage distribution were absent, the graphs in appendix IV would be smooth. While the graphs are smooth in some cases, in others there is a spike at the minimum wage, suggesting that the minimum wage affects the wage distribution in these countries. Table 4.1 summarizes which country-sectors show spikes at the minimum wage and which do not. The formal sector graphs have spikes in Brazil, Chile, Colombia, Ecuador, Nicaragua, Panama, Paraguay, Peru, and the República Bolivariana de Venezuela (left graph on each axis in appendix IV, top left cell in table 4.1), where there is a clustering of wages around the minimum wage (vertical line) suggesting that the minimum wage alters the formal sector wage distribution for some workers. It is not fully binding, as shown by the many observations to the left of the vertical line; those are the subminimum workers.[3] Given the few enforcement mechanisms in LAC, the effects of the minimum wage are likely due to other factors, including union pressures, efficiency wages, or a sense of fairness.

Table 4.1. Degree to Which the Minimum Wage Is Binding in Wage Employment in LAC and Year of Analysis, by Sector

	Mw is somewhat binding (spike at the minimum wage)	Mw is not binding (smooth wage distribution)
Formal wage sector	Brazil (1999)	Argentina (2000)
	Chile (2001)	Bolivia (1999)[a]
	Colombia (1999)	Costa Rica (1999)
	Ecuador (1998)	El Salvador (1998)[a]
	Guyana (1999)[b]	Guatemala (2000)[a]
	Nicaragua (2001)	Honduras (1999)[a]
	Panama (1998)	Jamaica (1998)[a]
	Paraguay (2000)	Mexico (1999)
	Peru (1999)	Uruguay (1998)
	Venezuela, R.B. de (1998)	
Informal wage sector	Brazil (1999)	Argentina (2000)
	Chile (2001)	Bolivia (1999)
	Colombia (1999)	Costa Rica (1999)
	Ecuador (1998)	Dominican Republic (1997)[a]
	El Salvador (1998)	Guatemala (2000)
	Mexico (1999)	Honduras (1999)
	Nicaragua (2001)	Jamaica (1998)
	Panama (1998)	Uruguay (1998)[a]
	Paraguay (2000)	
	Peru (1999)	
	Venezuela, R.B. de (1998)	

Source. Kristensen and Cunningham (2006).
a. The kernel density wage distributions show a spike, but the cdf (right graph) does not show a cliff, suggesting that the minimum wage "impacts" we see in the kernel density may be a statistical artifact.
b. Wage workers could not be identified as formal sector or informal sector.

Contrary to the assumption that minimum wage legislation is relevant only to the formal sector, the left graph of each figure in appendix II shows that it affects the informal wage distributions in more countries than it affects the formal sector wage distributions. In Brazil, Chile, Colombia, Ecuador, El Salvador, Mexico, Nicaragua, Panama, Paraguay, Peru, and the República Bolivariana de Venezuela, spikes are evident at the minimum wage in the informal sector wage distribution (left graph on each axis, bottom left cell in table 4.1).

The fact that minimum wages are somewhat binding in the informal sector may be due to various factors. From the labor supply side, the minimum may be a benchmark for "fair" wages. Foguel (1997) argues that workers value not only their absolute wage, but also the wage relative to others of similar skill level. Whereas the exact value of a comparator wage in the formal sector may not be measured easily, the value in terms of minimum wages may be estimated. On the demand side, employers may pay the number of minimum wages comparable to the formal sector market wage for a particular occupation so that their employees will not leave for a similar job in the formal sector, a kind of efficiency wage. Or the results may be a statistical artifact: as informal sector wages are lower than formal sector wages, the presence of more individuals in the lower part of the distribution—where the minimum wage tends to be—may lead to more of a "piling up" around the minimum wage in the informal sector than in the formal sector. Thus, minimum wages may be equally binding in both sectors, but the lower wages of informal sector workers may give an appearance of being more binding. The empirical evidence presented later in this chapter shows that this last explanation is not the case.

An increase in the minimum wage has a positive effect on formal and informal sector wages. Turning from graphs to more rigorous analysis, table 4.2 summarizes the findings of key studies that estimate the effects of a minimum wage increase on average wages. Appendix II presents a more detailed version of the table, including information on the methodology used by the authors, the data, the time period, and the estimated elasticities. Regardless of the methodology used in the study, the time period studied, or the country of study, a 10 percent increase in the minimum wage increases the mean wage by 1–6 percent. The increase is particularly strong for workers who earn near the minimum, similar to the findings in the OECD. Notably, the positive effects are detected for formal salaried, informal salaried, and self-employed workers across the region.[4]

Minimum Wage Policies Increase Wages throughout the Wage Distribution

Numeraire effects are observed in several countries in the Region. Spikes are detected at multiples of the minimum wage in various countries, suggesting that the minimum wage may be used as a benchmark for other wages. This was noted by Neri, Gonzaga, and Camargo (2000) for Brazil, where numeraire effects were shown up to six times the minimum wage for Brazil. Testing in additional countries shows that the phenomenon is more widespread than just Brazil. For example, figure 4.1 shows that the wage distribution has cliffs—as highlighted by the vertical lines—at 1.0, 1.5, 2.0, 3.0, and 4.0 times the minimum wage in Jamaica, and the same for Mexico.[5]

Rigorous analysis confirms the numeraire observations in the graphs. Whereas the OECD literature tells us that minimum wages will affect only

Table 4.2. Summary of Key Empirical Literature on the Effect of the Minimum Wage on Wages in Latin America

Country and years analyzed	MW effect on average wages[a]	Note	Source
Brazil 1984–99	+[b]	effects throughout the wage distribution	Fajnzylber (2002)
Brazil 1980–93	+, 0[c]	first half of period, second half of period	Carneiro and Faria (1997)
Brazil 1983–99	+[b]	bigger effect in the informal than formal	Foguel, Ramos, Carneiro (2001)
Brazil 1984–2000	+	throughout the wage distribution	Lemos (2002)
Brazil 1995–2001	+	only those clustered near the mw	Neumark, Cunningham, and Siga (2006)
Brazil 1996, 1999	+	only for poor near mw	Soares (2002)
Colombia 1997–2000	+[b]	throughout the wage distribution	Maloney and Nuñez (2004)
Colombia 1962–92	+	manufacturing sector only	Bell (1997)
Colombia 1984–2001	0 +[c]	lowest 40% of population, 40th–60th percentile of population	Arango and Pachón (2003)
Costa Rica 1980–96	+ − − 0[c]	formal sector, small firm, self-employed, part-time	Gindling and Terrell (2005)
Mexico 1988–98	+[b]	throughout the wage distribution	Cunningham and Siga (2006)
Mexico 1985–2001	+	formal sector only	Castellanos, Garcia-Verdu, & Kaplan (2004)
Mexico 1972–90	0	manufacturing sector only	Bell (1997)

Note: A description of the methodology and the elasticity estimates is given in appendix II.
a. A positive sign indicates a positive effect of a minimum wage increase on other wages, a negative sign indicates a negative effect of a minimum wage increase on other wages, and a 0 indicates that an increase in the minimum wage does not have any identifiable effect on average wages.
b. Effects for the formal and informal sectors, estimated separately.
c. Each sign corresponds to the group listed in the "Note" column, respectively.

the wages of those who earned at or below it (Brown 1999), in Latin America, they also affect wages above the minimum. Figure 4.2 gives the estimated percent increase in the hourly wages of Brazilian, Colombian, and Mexican workers in various parts of the wage distribution. An increase in the minimum wage has a positive effect on the wages of workers up to many multiples of the minimum wage. In Brazil, any increase in the

Figure 4.1. Cumulative Density Functions Showing "Spikes" at Multiples of the Minimum Wage

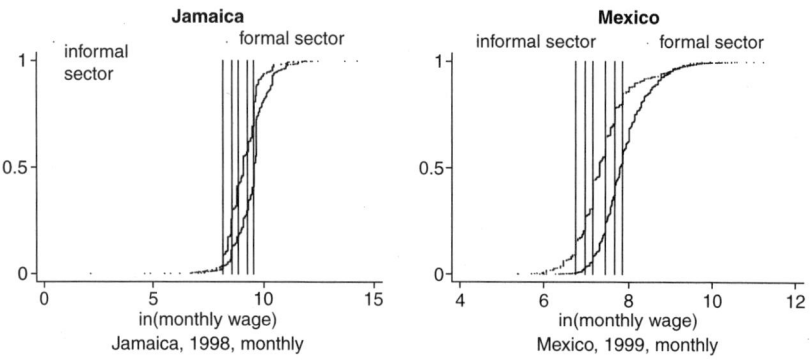

Jamaica, 1998, monthly

Mexico, 1999, monthly

Source: Kristensen and Cunningham (2006).
Note: The vertical lines for Jamaica are set at 1, 1.5, 2, 3 and 4 times the minimum wage. The vertical lines for Mexico are set at 1, 1.25, 1.5, 2, 2.5, and 3 times the minimum wage.

minimum wage is perfectly reflected in the wages of very poor Brazilian workers (earning one half to one minimum wage), with a smaller increase for those earning at the old minimum wage and yet smaller increases up to those earning six–nine minimum wages, until no effects are felt for those earning more than 9 minimum wages. The benefits of the minimum wage increase in Mexico run out at seven times the minimum wage (which is a much smaller monetary value than that in Brazil) whereas the only benefits in Colombia are experienced by workers at the 45th–60th wage centiles, who earn two–three minimum wages.

Similar to the argument for the reasons that minimum wage effects are observed in the informal sector, wage effects above the minimum may be due to the numeraire effect. Because of the history of the minimum wage as a price index during hyperinflationary periods in many countries, it may still be used to guide wage values throughout the wage distribution. Or it may be due to employers trying to maintain some level of fairness so as to maintain productivity levels among workers who earn above the minimum wage. Card and Krueger (1995), who found a similar result for low-wage workers in the United States, argue that the relative wages in a firm are important. If an increase in the minimum wage "sweeps up" those who had earned below the new minimum wage to levels earned by those who were "above minimum wage earners" before the increase, employers will increase the wages of the former "above minimum wage earners" a bit to maintain a gap between these workers and minimum

Figure 4.2. Average Wage Increase due to a 1% Increase in the Minimum Wage, by Position in the Wage Distribution before the Wage Change (Full-Time Workers), %

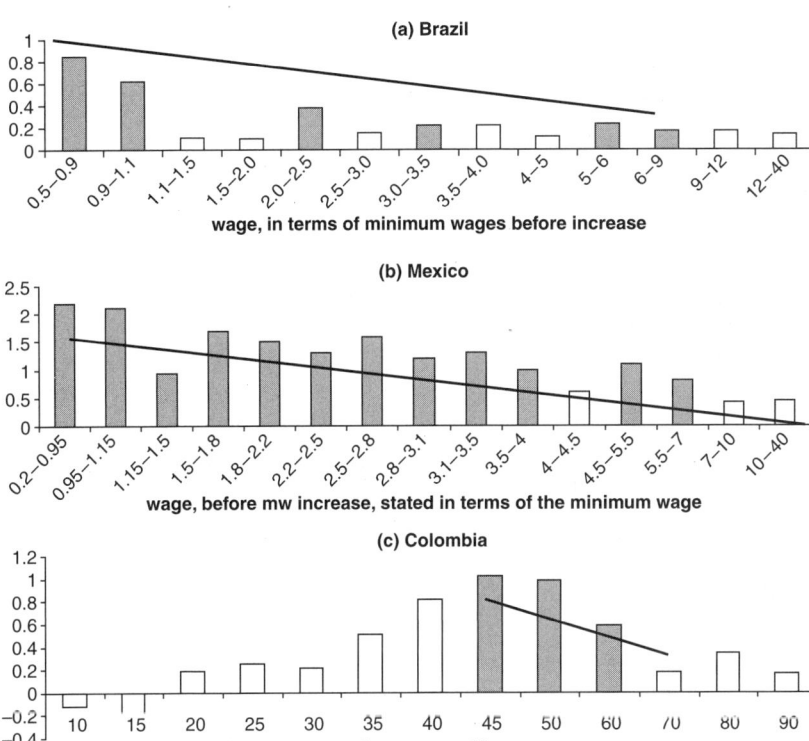

Source: Cunningham and Siga (2006) for Mexico and Brazil; Arango (2004) for Colombia.
Note: A colored bar indicates the coefficient is statistically significant at the 5% level, a white bar indicates that it is not.

wage workers, thus encouraging them to continue exerting a level of effort above the minimum effort.

The Level of the Minimum Wage Determines Whether It Increases or Decreases Wage Inequality

An increase in the minimum wage reduces wage inequality in countries with a low relative minimum wage. The downward-sloping curves of figures 4.2 (a) and (b) show that the lowest-paid workers have the greatest increase in wages when the minimum changes. Low-paid but above-the-minimum workers see their wages increase by a lesser amount, and workers at the top of the distribution do not see any change in their wages.

This results in compression of the wage distribution. Direct tests of the change in wage inequality using Brazilian (Lemos 2002, Angel-Urdinola and Wodon 2003, Soares 2002, Rodrigues and Menezes 2003), Colombian (Bell 1997), Argentine and Mexican (Rodrigues and Menezes 2003), and U.S. data (Neumark, Schweitzer, and Wascher 2000) show that wage inequality decreases with an increase in the minimum wage.[6] However, this cannot be generalized worldwide as no effect is found in the case of the United Kingdom, which has low relative minimum wages (Machin and Manning 1994).

However, the minimum wage can exacerbate wage inequality in high-minimum-wage countries. In Colombia, where the relative minimum wage is high, the benefits of the minimum wage skip over low-wage workers and raise the wages of those in the middle of the wage distribution. An increase in the minimum wage increases wages of those in the 45th to 60th wage deciles, with no effects on the lower or upper parts of the wage distribution. This implies that higher minimum wages increase wage inequality between the poor and middle-income workers (Arango and Pachón 2003).

Wage Benefits Are Not Concentrated on Any Particular Group of Workers

In Brazil and Mexico, youth and older adults, men and women, primary and secondary school, and formal and informal workers all benefit from wage increases. In Mexico, where the more vulnerable groups benefit from minimum wage increases, the "less vulnerable," such as men, formal sector workers, and the most educated, experience even larger wage gains than female, informal sector, or less educated workers. In Brazil, however, a clear pattern does not emerge. Some groups gain and others lose, but these gains continue up the wage distribution for all groups (Cunningham and Siga 2006).

An increase in the minimum wage causes greater gains for men's wages than for women's wages. In Mexico and Brazil, both women and men benefit from a higher minimum wage, but the gains are greater for men throughout the wage distribution. Although the distribution of women's wages shows sharper spikes than men's wages (Soares 2001, and Rodrigues and Filho 2003), indicating that more women are clustered around the minimum wage, women's wages do not necessarily respond to a change in the minimum wage to a greater degree than men's wages. Figure 4.3 shows that except for the lowest earners, men's

Figure 4.3. Mexico, Average Wage Increase due to a 1% Increase in the Minimum Wage, %

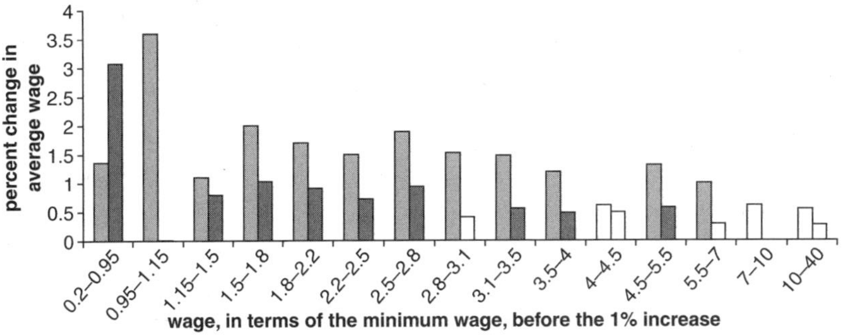

Source: Cunningham and Siga (2006).
Note: The percent increase for men is given in the left bar and for women in the right bar. A solid bar indicates the coefficient is statistically significant at the 5% level; a white bar indicates that it is not.

gains exceed women's at all wage levels in Mexico. Thus, while women are overrepresented among minimum-wage earners, their wages are less responsive to increases in the minimum. A 10 percent increase in the Mexican minimum wage led to a 10–36 percent increase in men's wages, but was responsible for only a 0–10 percent increase in women's wages (figure 4.3).[7] The minimum wage premium to men also appears in Brazil, where men enjoy a 0–14 percent increase in wages from a 10 percent increase in the minimum, whereas women experience gains equivalent to 0–6.5 percent (Cunningham and Siga 2006).

As in the OECD countries, young workers with low wages gain from an increase in the level of the minimum. However, unlike the OECD, adults whose wages are clustered around the minimum make even more significant wage gains. A 10 percent increase in the minimum wage in Mexico results in a 10 percent increase in the wages of youth who earn the minimum wage, but a 23 percent increase in the wages of adults in the same initial earnings groups. The differences between the age groups are much smaller in Brazil. Also, unlike OECD countries, wage gains are experienced by youth (and adults) with initial earnings that are above the minimum wage.

Workers with only a primary or secondary education benefit from higher minimum wages. In both Mexico and Brazil, a 10 percent increase in the minimum wage leads to an increase in wages as high as 7 percent in Brazil and 23 percent in Mexico for low- to medium-skilled workers. Brazilian workers with no formal schooling (not estimated for Mexico) do not benefit.

Table 4.3. Change in the Wage-Gini Coefficient (by Demographic Group) due to a Decrease in the Minimum Wage, 1988–99

	Brazil ($\Delta mw = -8.6\%$)		Mexico ($\Delta mw = -37.7\%$)	
	Δ Gini due to change in the minimum wage	% of change in Gini explained by the change in the minimum wage	Δ Gini due to change in the minimum wage	% of change in Gini explained by the change in the minimum wage
Men	0.02	10.7	0.02	29.3
Women	0.01	5.6	0.05	59
Unskilled	0.02	9.3	0.05	51.9
Skilled	0.01	7.9	0.03	40
Young	0.00	0	0.04	58
Adults	0.02	13.7	0.03	47.4
Formal	−0.01	4.8	0.01	7
Informal	−0.03	18.4	0.05	37.3

Source: Souza Rodrigues and Menezes Filho (2003).
Note: Assume no unemployment effects and no numeraire effects.

The decrease in the real minimum wage across the Region since the 1980s is partly responsible for the increased dispersion in the wage distribution of women and youth. The findings of this section are supported by another exercise that simulates the change in the Gini coefficient (a measure of inequality) owing to a decrease in the real value of the minimum wage in the 1990s.[8] Table 4.3 shows that when the minimum wage decreases, the dispersion of wages increases 5–59 percent among men, women, unskilled, skilled, and adults in both Mexico and Brazil. The effects are particularly strong for the wage distributions of women, the unskilled, and the informal sector. Thus, increased minimum wages would decrease the inequality in these countries, as suggested by figure 4.2. Unfortunately, the "high relative wage" case of Colombia was not estimated.

Minimum Wages Increase Unemployment

An increase in the minimum wages causes job loss. Throughout the Region, and regardless of year or methodology used for the analysis, an increase in the minimum wage results in higher unemployment and lower employment (table 4.4). The effects may be very small (Lemos (2002) for Brazil) or substantial (Bell (1997) for Colombia), with most countries experiencing a job loss of 2 percent for a 10 percent increase in the minimum wage. As with the wage impacts, job loss occurs most among those

Table 4.4. Summary of Key Literature on the Effect of the Minimum Wage on Unemployment and Employment in Latin America

Country	Effect[a]	Note	Source
Unemployment			
Brazil 1982–87	+[b]		Foguel (1997)
Brazil 1982–99	+[b]	especially in the informal sector	Fajnzylber (2002)
Brazil 1996–2001	+[b]	informal wage sector only	Cunningham and Siga (2006)
Chile 1957–96	+	and increases the duration of unemployment	Montenegro (2003)
Colombia 1997–99	+[b]	throughout the wage distribution; more in formal than s.e. sector	Maloney and Nuñez (2004)
Mexico 1983–2000	0[b]	positive if time and state controls not included	Garza Cantu and Bazaldua (2001)
Mexico 1988–98	0	no strong effects in the formal or informal	Cunningham and Siga (2006)
Employment			
Brazil 1982–87	–[b]	decline in number employed and increase in labor market exit	Foguel (1997)
Brazil 1982–2000	+[b]	small effects	Lemos (2002)
Brazil 1995, 1999	–, +[c]	formal, informal	Carneiro and Corseuil (2001)
Brazil 1982–2001	–, +[c]	formal, informal	Foguel, Ramos, and Carneiro (2001); Carneiro (2000)
Brazil 1996–2001	–, +[c]	household heads, household dependents	Neumark, Cunningham, and Siga (2006)
Colombia 1980–87	+	manufacturing employment only	Bell (1997)
Colombia 1984–2001	–, +[c]	household heads, dependents	Arango and Pachón (2003)
Costa Rica 1980–96	+, –[c]	full-time workers, part-time workers	Gindling and Terrell (2005)
Mexico 1984–90	0	manufacturing employment only	Bell (1997)

Source: Cited in last column of table.
Note: For full details, see appendix II.
a. A positive sign indicates a positive effect of a minimum wage increase on employment and unemployment, a negative sign indicates a negative effect of a minimum wage increase on employment and unemployment, and a zero indicates that an increase in the minimum wage does not have any identifiable effect on employment and unemployment.
b. Effects for the formal and informal sectors, estimated separately.
c. Each sign corresponds to the group listed in the "Note" column, respectively.

who earned near the old minimum wage, but is felt further up the wage distribution as well (Cunningham and Siga (2006) for Brazil; Maloney and Nuñez (2004), Arango and Pachón (2003) for Colombia). The only country analyzed for which no job loss was detected was Mexico, where the authors argue that the minimum wage is too low to have any impact on the labor market (Bell 1997).

The minimum wage causes unemployment among formal sector workers, but the evidence is mixed for the informal sector.[9] In Brazil and Colombia, an increase in the minimum wage corresponds to a lower likelihood of retaining one's job in the formal sector. The implications for informal sector employment are not as clear (table 4.4). Some Colombian and Brazilian literature find the expected disemployment effects, since the minimum wage appears to be binding in the informal sector, but other studies in Brazil show an *employment* effect in the informal sector (Carneiro and Corseuil 2001; Corseuil and Morgado 2000; Foguel, Ramos, and Carneiro 2001; Carneiro 2000). These authors argue that higher minimum wages force formal sector workers into informal sector jobs. No employment effects in either sector were detected in Mexico, with its low minimum wage, even though the minimum wage is somewhat binding.

An increase in the minimum wage leads to greater job loss among women, youth, and low-skilled workers.[10] Although wage gains are shared by most in the population, with greater gains among the less skilled, job loss is less equally shared. In Brazil (Cunningham and Siga 2006), an increase in the minimum wage leads to greater job loss for women, youth, and low-skilled workers whose wages are clustered around the minimum. No job loss is experienced by men, prime-aged or older workers, and the high-skilled. In Mexico, a pattern is not discernible, which is not surprising given the lack of evidence of job loss in the aggregate.

Caution should be taken in applying these results to all countries in LAC, since the findings are for only two countries, one with a low relative minimum wage but strong numeraire effects (Mexico) and the other for a country with a moderate relative minimum wage and some numeraire effects (Brazil). The extent to which the minimum wage supports certain segments of the labor force depends on how high the minimum wage is relative to market wages of various demographic groups. For example, in countries with a very low minimum wage relative to the wage of low-skilled workers, minimum wages are very binding for those with primary school or less, as shown in chapter 3. The minimum wage may be too low to be meaningful for more highly skilled workers. However, in economies with a relatively high minimum wage, such as Paraguay and Ecuador, the wage distribution of the more highly skilled is most affected; the wage distribution of workers with a secondary education is affected more than that of workers with primary school or less.

Subnational Minimum Wages Are Standard Practice

A national minimum wage is generally not feasible because of regional price variation. Although national minimum wages may officially exist in most countries, heterogeneity in labor markets across a country creates multiple real regional minimum wages. For example, even though Brazil eliminated its regional nominal minimum wages in 1984, figure 4.4 shows that the real minimum wage variation by region still exists. The plots of the wage distribution in the different regions of Brazil in 1999 clearly show that the national minimum wage is too low to be relevant in the wealthy state of São Paulo, whereas it appears to play a role in the poorer state of Bahia. In real terms, the minimum wage, although identical in nominal terms, is, in fact, regionally specific.

Figure 4.4. Kernal Density and Cumulative Density Plots of Wages, by Region

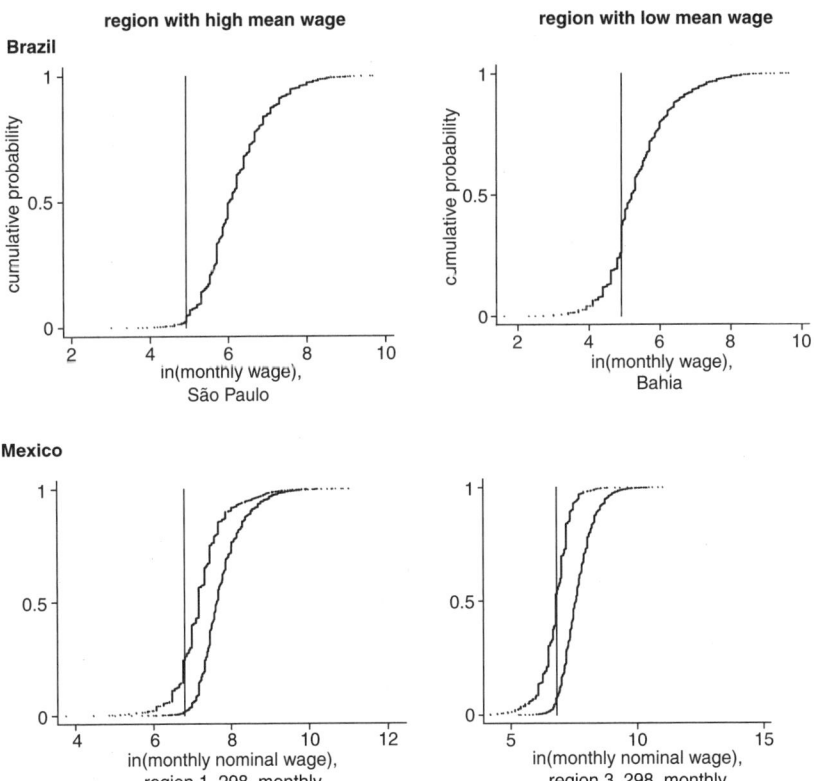

Source: Author's calculations from PNAD (2001; Brazil) and ENEU (1998; second semester, Mexico).
Note: Vertical line is minimum wage. Mexico: left-hand curve is informal sector; right-hand curve is formal sector.

Mexico has multiple regional-specific minimum wages that allow for regional variation in labor markets. Although the minimum wage is low across Mexico, the minimumå wage in region 1, if applied to region 3, would have much bigger implications for employment and wages in region 3 than does the lower minimum wage applied to region 3. By setting different nominal minimum wages for regions, a national "real" minimum wage exists, so that the impacts are similar across the country (figure 4.4).

One of the often voiced concerns about regional minimum wages is that they give incentives for migration from low to high nominal minimum wage regions. A counterexample is the United States, in which each state chooses to use the federal minimum wage or to set a higher level, resulting in a high variance in minimum wages across the country. The state-level minimum wages have not been shown to create an incentive for migration from low- into high-minimum wage states, because the real minimum wage varies less than the nominal wage (Brown 1999).

Notes

1. The methodology presented by DiNardo, Fortin, and Lemieux (1996) and Maloney and Nuñez (2004) is used rather than the probability density function (pdf). Kernel density plots are estimated for each country-sector combination. They are basically a continuous version of discrete histograms; that is, they smooth a line between each observation x_i along the x-axis or group of observations within a certain bandwidth of the x-axis to obtain an estimated density. We also present the cumulative density plots (cdf) as they do not require any assumptions about bandwidths, thus giving an alternative illustration of the wage distribution. For the cdf, a "cliff" would correspond to the "spike" in the kernel density plot. For full discussion of the methodology, see Kristensen and Cunningham (2006).

2. To control for measurement errors introduced by part-time workers in countries where monthly minimum wages are legislated, the analysis is confined to "full-time employees," defined as individuals working 30–50 hours weekly who are not in the self-employment sector.

3. The spikes in the graphs may be a result of employers who reward or respondents who report a round number. In Chile and the República Bolivariana de Venezuela, with a minimum wage of 100,000 pesos monthly, this may be the case, but in the other countries, the minimum wage is not a round number, so the evidence of the role of the minimum wage in distorting the wage distribution is more compelling.

4. The differences in the estimated elasticities from different studies of the same country are due to different methodologies, segments of the labor market

studied, and the period studied. The latter is particularly important in Brazil, since the hyperinflationary period and wage indexing during the 1980s may have created a spurious correlation between wages and the minimum wage.

5. Although the minimum wage in Jamaica is J$800 dollars per week, the cliffs are not noted for every multiple of 100. The minimum wage in Mexico was Mexi $888 monthly. The surveys for which this phenomenon is noted do not use the minimum wage as a response in their surveys. Instead, an actual currency value of wages or income is recorded.

6. Lemos (2002) finds that a 10 percent increase in the Brazilian minimum wage reduces the wage gap between the 50th and 90th centiles by 34 percent and the gap between the 10th and 90th centiles by 15 percent. Neumark, Schweitzer, and Wascher (2000) find that an increase in the minimum wage increases the wage of those earning less than two minimum wages in the short run, with no long-term effects. Angel-Urdinola and Wodon (2003) find a decrease in the Gini coefficient by 0.0033–0.0037 percentage points for a 6 percent increase in the minimum wage in Brazil.

7. The lowest wage category has a particularly large minimum wage effect. This phenomenon has been observed in the other studies that use this methodology (Neumark, Schweitzer, and Wascher [2004] for the United States, Maloney and Nuñez [2004] for Colombia), that attribute the particularly high impacts to mismeasurement.

8. The author constructs a counterfactual distribution of the wage distribution in 1999, if the real minimum wages, characteristics of the labor force, and unobserved characteristics in 1988 had not changed. The difference in the Gini can then be attributed to each of these characteristics. For a full discussion of the methodology, see appendix I.

9. An increase in unemployment is not synonymous with a decrease in employment, since a higher minimum wage may induce labor force entry, thus increasing the unemployment rate.

10. "Young" are defined as workers age 16–24, "prime-aged" are age 25–50, and older workers are age 51–65. "Unskilled" are those with no more than a primary education ("no school" are omitted), "semiskilled" are those with no more than a secondary education, and "skilled" are those with a university education.

CHAPTER 5

The Households: The Minimum Wage as an Antipoverty Tool

Chapter 4 showed that minimum wages generally have a positive effect on the wage distribution and a negative effect on employment. Ultimately, though, we are concerned with the impact of the minimum wage on poverty. This requires us to shift our unit of analysis from the individual worker to the household for two reasons. First, households pool income so the net effect of the minimum wage on household earnings is more relevant than the effect on the labor status or earning of an individual within the household.[1] Second, poverty is measured at the level of the household, not the individual. By examining the level of the minimum wage relative to household needs and the effect of the minimum wage on household income, we will have a better understanding of the usefulness of the minimum wage as an antipoverty tool.

This section is concerned with three questions. First, it determines whether the minimum wage is a viable household poverty reduction tool. Second, it aggregates the gains and losses across households and determines the net impact of an increase in the minimum wage on households at different parts of the income distribution. Finally, it identifies which households win and which households lose when the minimum wage increases.

The Value of the Minimum Wage Is Below the Household Subsistence Level

The minimum wage exceeds the US$2 daily poverty line for most countries. If the objective of the minimum wage is to guarantee that all workers, regardless of productivity level, receive a living wage, a good benchmark for the "fairness" of the minimum is its level relative to the poverty line—that is, the minimum income necessary to purchase basic good and services. In 17 of the 20 countries studied, the minimum wage exceeds the crude US$2 per day (PPP-adjusted) poverty line (figure 5.1). In Paraguay, the minimum wage is equivalent to more than nine times the PPP-adjusted US$2 per daily poverty line, whereas in the República Bolivariana de Venezuela, Mexico, and Uruguay, it is less than this poverty line.

Figure 5.1. Minimum Wage Relative to the Household per Capita Poverty Lines—US$2 per Day or the Consumption-Basket Poverty Line

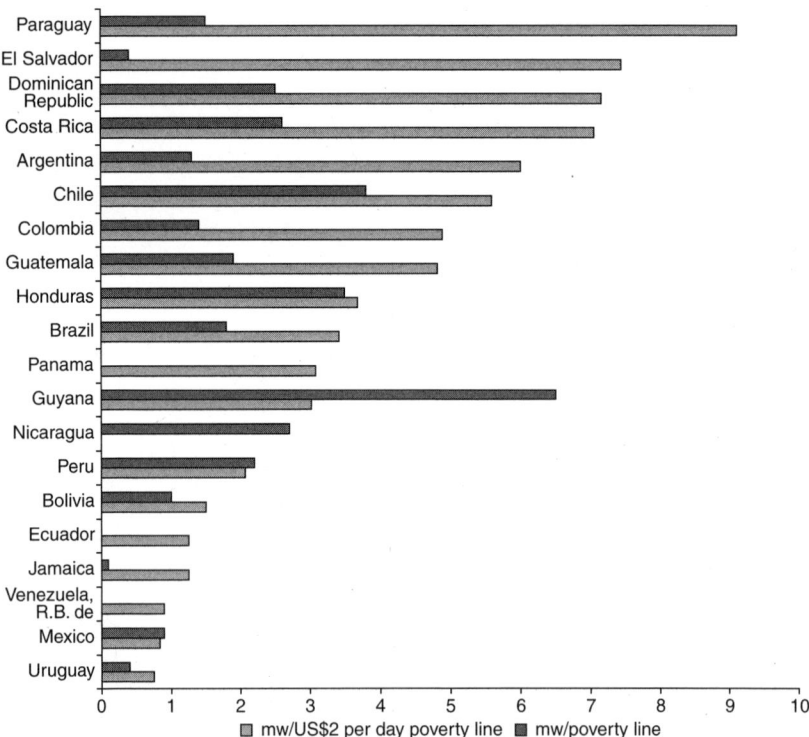

Source: Kristensen and Cunningham (2006).

The "basic goods" poverty measure gives similar conclusions.[2] Although the value of the basic goods basket is generally lower than the PPP-adjusted $2 per day, the minimum wage is still above the poverty line in all countries except Jamaica, Uruguay, Mexico, and El Salvador (figure 5.1). Thus, for both poverty measures, the minimum wage seems sufficient to meet the minimum needs of the individual.

The minimum wage is not sufficient to meet household consumption needs. Much minimum wage legislation in Latin America states that the minimum should be sufficient to cover the needs of the family (Starr 1981). If the worker's income also must provide for the needs of household dependents, the minimum wage falls far short: in households with one dependent per worker, the minimum wage can provide the basic subsistence (basic goods basket) in only 7 of the 17 sampled countries (Peru, Nicaragua, Dominican Republic, Honduras, Guyana, Chile, and Costa Rica). And in households with one minimum-wage earner and three dependents, the level of the minimum wage is only sufficient to provide income above the poverty line in Guyana, and perhaps in Chile and Honduras.[3]

The Minimum Wage Decreases Poverty Rates but Does Not Help the Most Poor

There is very little evidence in LAC about the impacts of the minimum wage on household poverty and inequality (table 5.1).[4] Two studies in the mid-1990s used aggregate country data and found that higher minimum wages have some poverty-increasing effects and some poverty-decreasing effects (Lustig and McLeod 1996, Morley 1992). More careful simulations using Brazilian microdata found that an increase in the minimum wage has no effects on poverty, after taking into account the unemployment effects of a minimum wage increase (IPEA 2000). Similarly, a direct test of how an increase in the minimum wage affects the poverty status of U.S. families also finds no effects (Neumark and Wascher 1997). However, the U.S. paper does find that an increase in the minimum wage increases the wages of the poorest, not by enough to bring them above the poverty line but enough to have a significant effect.

In countries where the minimum wage causes unemployment, the poorest do not benefit from higher minimum wages; instead, the benefits are concentrated among those households near the poverty line. In Colombia, the poorest households—those in the bottom 25 percent of the household income distribution—neither gain nor lose from higher

Table 5.1. Review of the Key Literature Examining the Impact of the Minimum Wage on Household Poverty and Inequality in Latin America

Country	Poverty/inequality impact of an increase in the mw	Note	Source
Poverty			
Household-level data			
Brazil 1997	0	household-level data	IPEA (2000)
Colombia 1997–2001	–	household-level data	Arango and Pachon (2003)
Mexico 1988–99	–	household-level data	Cunningham and Siga (2006)
United States 1986–95	0	household-level data	Neumark and Wascher (1997)
Aggregate estimates			
Asia, Africa, LAC 1950–80	–		Lustig and McLeod (1996)
Latin America 1981–89	+, –[a]	recovery, recessions	Morley (1992)
Inequality			
Brazil 1995–2001	+	indirect test, only losses for poor	Neumark, Cunningham, and Siga (forthcoming)
Colombia 1984–2001	0, +[a]	direct test, short run, long run	Arango and Pachon (2003)
Mexico 1988–98	–	indirect test, faster gains among poorest households	Cunningham and Siga (2006)

a. Each sign corresponds to the group listed in the Note column, respectively.

minimum wages. As only households with labor income are included in the sample, this suggests that either the wage and unemployment effects balance each other out in this sample—some households gain while others lose in equal proportions—or that the minimum wage laws do not have any effects on this segment of the wage-earning population. The latter explanation is more likely, since, as shown in chapter 4, the high minimum wages in Colombia pass over workers in the bottom half of the wage distribution. Only households in the middle of the household income distribution—25th to 80th centiles—benefit from an increase in the minimum wage. The poverty line is in the 50th centile of the wage distribution, so poverty rates may change, but this is due to increases in household income among the better-off poor families

(Arango 2004). Box 5.1 summarizes the methodologies used to test minimum wage effects on household poverty.

Mexico presents the case where the minimum wage, although low, increases household earnings among the poor. The workers analysis for Mexico showed positive wage gains, especially among the poor, and no unemployment shocks (chapter 4). When taking the household as the unit of observation, the poorest households experience the highest wage gains following an increase in the minimum wage (figure 5.2). The gains are concentrated among households that earn up to one minimum wage per capita. Notably, these are the very poorest, so there are still many poor Mexicans who do not benefit from the minimum wage increase (Cunningham and Siga 2006), and the effects on the poverty rate are likely to be negligible.

The Brazil case demonstrates the dynamic poverty effects of the minimum wage, where short-run gains are offset by long-run losses. On average, the higher minimum wage has a positive short-run effect on very poor families, those in the bottom 30 percent of the household income distribution when wages increase. But in the long run, once labor contracts expire and workers are fired, the net effect is a loss of household income per capita among poor families. In other words, the income loss

---

Box 5.1

Methodology for Testing the Minimum Wage Effects on Household Poverty and Inequality

The findings of this section are surprising: there is no previous literature from Latin America and little from the OECD to corroborate findings. Thus, two general methodologies were used to ensure that the findings were robust. The methodologies are defined in detail in appendix I, but in summary they are as follows:

- Using short panel data (small t, large n), household income levels are tracked before and after minimum wage changes. The variation in the minimum wage (also, the mw/median wage was used) is correlated with changes in household income (used for Colombia and Mexico).
- Cross-section time series methods were used to examine the correlation between wage movements at different income centiles and variations in the minimum wages over long periods (big t, small n). Aggregating across households, the effects of the minimum wage on different population groups are estimated (used for Brazil and Colombia).

Figure 5.2. Impact of a 10% Increase in the Minimum Wage on Household Income in Mexico, 1999

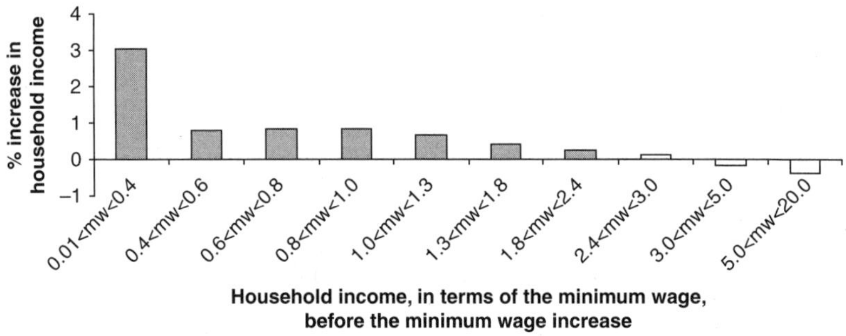

Household income, in terms of the minimum wage, before the minimum wage increase

Source: Cunningham and Siga (2006).

Note: The shaded bars indicate that an impact was found (t-values are statistically significant at the 5% level); the nonshaded bars indicate that a change was estimated, but we cannot determine whether it is the measured amount or zero (t-values are not significant at the 5% level).

among poor households where a worker loses a job is greater than the gains among households where wage increase dominates. The loss is small in monetary terms (approximately 8 reais, equivalent to US$2.50), but this is a group average, so the monetary value should be interpreted as meaning the particular minimum wage policy in Brazil causes more losers than winners among the poor. The wage gains among the poor observed in an earlier chapter are wiped out by job loss (Neumark, Cunningham, and Siga 2006). This should have negligible effects on the country's poverty rate, thus supporting the earlier simulations (IPEA 2000).

High Minimum Wages Increase Household Income Inequality

If minimum wages are relatively high, an increase can exacerbate income inequalities. A direct test of the gap between household incomes at different points of the wage distribution shows that an adjustment in the minimum wage increases the spread between the poorest households and the rest of the distribution in Colombia. The gap between the poorest (lowest 25 percent of the population) and the median or 70th percentile increased with an increase in the minimum wage. What appears to be happening is that very poor households remain poor, whereas the rest of the population, particularly those workers whose wages are clustered around the minimum wage, gains. The households that are left behind are those in which workers whose wages we would expect to be affected by the minimum wage are not (Arango and Pachón 2003).

Minimum wages that create unemployment can also exacerbate income distributions. Direct tests of the inequality impacts have not been estimated for Brazil and Mexico, but we can extrapolate from the findings to formulate conclusions regarding the income distribution effects of the minimum wage in economies where the minimum wage affects the wages and employment of very poor workers. As discussed previously, the poorest Brazilian households become even poorer when the minimum wage increases, whereas the other 70 percent of the distribution stays the same, thus stretching the household income distribution and increasing income inequality. In Mexico, where the poor gain the most from minimum wage increases because of the absence of unemployment effects, household income inequality should decline since income increases were observed in the bottom of the distribution, with no change higher up the distribution. Thus, the household income distribution is compressed. The Mexico result is consistent with evidence in the United States, where an increase in the minimum wage increases the well-being of the poorest families and has little effect on those on the rest of the income distribution.

In sum, the effect of the minimum wage on the poor will depend on the relative level of the minimum wage and the nature of wage and labor contracts. The level of the minimum wage is important, since a minimum wage that is relatively high will increase wages of the less poor while creating unemployment among the poorest, as demonstrated by the Colombia case. Conversely, a low minimum wage, as in the case of Mexico, will cause a modest increase in wages among the poorest while avoiding unemployment effects. However, the low minimum wage is also too low to lift households above the poverty line. Thus, the policy maker must determine whether a small wage increase—through a low minimum-wage level—is sufficient, or if higher standards should be set to benefit some, even though others will experience the perverse effects of the minimum wage. The long-run effects are also important to keep in mind: wages can adjust very rapidly, thus decreasing poverty, but employment status adjusts in the longer run. Thus, the nature of labor contracts can determine the extent to which benefits of minimum wage hikes are enjoyed.

Notes

1. Aggregating the change in income for all workers does not give us a very good idea of the poverty impacts as individuals often benefit from the labor income of others in the household. Such pooling of household income may diminish

the negative effects to the individual of a job loss if he or she can draw on the wages of others in the household who may have benefited from a minimum wage increase. For example, literature from the United States shows that although a minimum wage increase has a positive effect on income and no effect on unemployment, it does little to reduce household poverty since minimum wage earners tend to be teenage workers who contribute little to the household income (Burkhauser, Couch, and Wittenburg 1996).

2. The basic goods basket contains the foodstuff necessary to meet the minimum daily caloric intake of a person (adjusted for sex and age) and the necessary clothing, shelter, and other basic necessities for a minimum standard of living. The value of this basket may be used as a poverty line, whereas the value of only the food portion of the basket may be used to identify the indigent poor.

3. These calculations assume that children require the same daily consumption rates as adults. This assumption was used to simplify the analysis, but more careful analysis can be conducted by estimating the average household structure in each country, estimating the income needed so that such a family is at the poverty line, and then comparing the minimum wage level to that income.

4. The poverty line is a somewhat arbitrary cutoff, particularly in this case where we do not have the information to appropriately weight households and assign the monetary value of the baskets accordingly, and where we do not have information on nonlabor income. Thus, the term "poverty" is used loosely in this chapter.

CHAPTER 6

The State: The Minimum Wage Implications for Public Expenditures

An increase in the minimum wage affects LAC fiscal accounts. In LAC, the governments employ a large labor force, social assistance payments are tied to the minimum wage, and the minimum is used as an eligibility criterion for participation in public assistance programs in many countries. These factors place a fiscal burden on the governments, thus potentially tempering the impulse to raise the minimum wage, but also restricting the degree to which it can be used as a social protection instrument.[1]

The Minimum Wage May Have Large Impacts on the Public Sector Wage Bill

The minimum wage can have a large effect on the government's wage bill, especially if there are numeraire effects. Simulations for five distinct countries in the Region show that a 20 percent increase in the minimum wage can range from no impact to a very large impact on government accounts (see box 6.1 for a brief description of the methodology).[2] Assuming no unemployment effects in the public sector as the minimum wage increases, an increase of 20 percent in the wages of those at the minimum wage will increase the wage bill by up to 7.1 percent (table 6.1). When taking into consideration the numeraire effect that is evident for

Box 6.1

Methodology for Simulations

To estimate the impact of an increase in the minimum wage on the government's wage bill, a three-step process was used.

First, the impacts of the minimum wage on public sector wages were estimated using kernel density plots, identifying where the minimum wage was binding and numeraire effects.

Second, a 20 percent increase in the minimum wage was assumed and applied to (a) minimum wage earners and (b) minimum wage earners and those earning multiples of the minimum wage.

Third, the total simulated wage bill was calculated based on the size of the public sector, the number of employees affected by the minimum wage, and their new incomes. The amount of the increase relative to total public expenditures was calculated.

For the detailed methodology, see appendix I.

Table 6.1. Increase in the Public Sector Wage Bill due to a 20 Percent Increase in the Minimum Wage, by Percentage

	Brazil	Colombia	Dominican Republic	Mexico	Panama
Assuming wages at or below the minimum wage are affected					
Wage bill	0.2	7.1	0.2	0.0	3.6
Current expenditures	0.03	1.4	0.08	0.0	1.4
Total expenditures	0.02	1.1	0.06	0.0	1.3
Including those who benefit from numeraire effects					
Wage bill	0.2	10.3	2.2	0.0	8.0
Current expenditures	0.05	2.5	2.0	0.0	5.2
Total expenditures	0.02	1.6	0.8	0.0	2.8

Source: Guzman, Lizardo, and Lora (2003).

public sector wages, the wage bill increases by even more, to 10.3 percent in Colombia, 8.0 percent in Panama, and 2.2 percent in the Dominican Republic (fourth row in table 6.1).[3] The increase in total expenditure is as high as 2.8 percent in Panama, owing to the relatively large size of the public sector.

The degree to which the minimum wage affects the public sector deficit largely depends on how binding the minimum wage is in the public sector. The minimum wage does not necessarily affect the public sector in all countries. Mexico's very low minimum wage is not binding, so even a 20 percent increase in the wage will have no effect on the wage bill or total expenditures. However, in countries with very binding public sector minimum wages, such as Colombia, the impacts are quite large.

The wage effects are greatest for local government. Since wages are lower in local government, and the workforce is larger, an increase in the minimum wage will have larger impacts at the local level than the federal level. A study in Brazil (IPEA 2000a) showed that a 10 percent increase in the minimum wage in Brazil would increase the federal government's payroll by 0.03 percent—since virtually no one earns the minimum or close to it—to an increase in the municipal level payroll by 1.3 percent, where 13 percent of the workers earn at or near the minimum.

An Increase in the Minimum Wage Can Have Substantial Impacts on the Cost of Social Benefits

The value of social benefits is tied to the minimum wage in many LAC countries, leading to large fiscal account implications for minimum wage increases. In Brazil, an increase of the minimum wage by $100 reais (equivalent to US$30, 2003 values), or 40 percent, would increase pension expenses 13 times more than it would increase revenues, leading to an increased deficit in the social security system of R$160 million (IPEA 2000b).

The link between the minimum wage and other public program payments, although less than the impact of pension payments, is still significant. Examples include:

- *shock benefits to workers* that are indexed to the minimum wage, including payments for a death in the family (Ecuador); funeral grants (Argentina, Bolivia, Chile, Colombia, Ecuador); weddings, prenatal and birth benefits (Bolivia, Jamaica); illness benefits, unemployment insurance (Argentina, Brazil, Uruguay); and disability or survivor pensions (Brazil, Colombia, Costa Rica, Ecuador, Jamaica)
- *stipends paid to participants in job training programs*, particularly youth (Costa Rica, Mexico, Colombia)
- *wage bonuses*, including the "13th wage" (many countries)
- *public works programs* that index the wage to the minimum wage (Colombia, Argentina)

- *tax exemptions* or indexation (Mexico, Paraguay)
- *price of subsidized services* (the República Bolivariana de Venezuela).

In addition, family earnings relative to the minimum wage are used as criteria for participation in some social programs. If the minimum wage increases more than the average wage, the demand for social programs will increase. Examples include:

- *housing benefits* (Colombia, Costa Rica, El Salvador, Mexico)
- *food stamps* (Jamaica)
- *social protection schemes* (Brazil).

More indirectly, an increase in the minimum wage will increase expenditures in employment-related social programs. Since a higher minimum wage leads to unemployment, particularly among the poor, there will be a greater demand for programs that protect the income of the unemployed, such as public workfare, subsidized credit, and unemployment insurance.

The Chilean government has recognized the fiscal difficulties created by tying the minimum wage level to other social benefits. In response, it created "nonwage" minimum wages, which are used for these indexing purposes only. A separate "wage" minimum wage is used to affect labor market wages.

Although a higher minimum wage may increase government expenditures, it can also add to government coffers. As shown earlier, the minimum wage will have positive wage effects on some of the population, so additional revenue may come in the form of higher collections on labor taxes, which are a function of the wage, and government fees, which are indexed to the minimum wage in some countries.

In sum, the net effects on government accounts may be positive or negative, depending on the size of social programs and efficiency of tax collection. However, the expenditures on the low-wage earners are likely to outweigh the increase on tax collection among this group. Thus, there is a redistribution of income from poor workers, who experience greatest wage gains as the minimum wage increases, to poor nonworkers who are the recipients of public programs tied to the value of the minimum wage.

Notes

1. This section is largely based on Guzman, Lizardo, and Lora (2003).
2. The minimum wage is strongly binding for public sector employees in Panama, Brazil, and Colombia, but not in the Dominican Republic or Mexico. It covers

0.6 percent (Mexico) to 19.7 percent (Colombia) of public sector employees, with greater coverage for women in Brazil, Mexico, and the Dominican Republic, and for men in Panama and Colombia. Numeraire effects are quite strong at different parts of the wage distribution in all countries except Mexico.

3. This may be overestimated for Colombia because of the practice of subminimum increases for employees earning more than the minimum wage.

CHAPTER 7

The International Community: Lessons from Their Experiences

Heterogeneity in minimum wage institutions is not limited to LAC. Across the world, the number of minimum wages, coverage, minimum wage–setting mechanisms, and enforcement mechanisms differ. For example, Italy and Germany have hundreds of "minimum wages," which are negotiated and enforced by unions under a strong contract law framework. Australia's former system, which had hundreds of minimum wages, was part of a larger labor "awards system" that specified all remuneration for job types by states. In the United States, the federal minimum wage may be increased by the state minimum wage: state inspectors are responsible for enforcement. In Japan, each prefecture has its own minimum wage, which is recommended by a council composed of public interest groups, worker representatives, and employer representatives.

Although this report has shown that among a small group of countries, the net benefit of the minimum on household poverty in LAC is zero or negative, improving the design and complementing it with other social protection mechanisms perhaps can render the minimum wage a useful social protection tool. The diverse institutions in other regions of the world may offer clues to institutional designs that could improve the effectiveness of Latin America's minimum wage institutions. This chapter lays out examples of institutional designs that may be useful to LAC policy makers in improving the institutions in their own countries.

Setting and Managing Minimum Wages

There is no international consensus on the process for setting, adjusting, and enforcing minimum wages. The experiences across the world are varied and highlight the positive and negative aspects of the various lessons. Importantly, though, there is no clear process or guidelines that can be applied to minimum wage institutions in all countries. Instead, parameters differ by countries and need be retrofitted to meet the needs of a particular situation.

Before determining the criteria and parameters of minimum wage setting and adjustments, policy makers must decide on the objective of their minimum wage. As discussed in box 2.1, there are many motivations for creating a minimum wage, including protecting the most vulnerable, ensuring fair wages across the economy, creating a safety net, and promoting macroeconomic growth and stability, among others. Once this objective is determined, identification of the parameters becomes more straightforward.

The criteria for the level of the minimum wage are easy to define but difficult to quantify. Experiences across the world show that the criteria to set the level of the minimum wage are often a combination of social needs, ability to pay, equity, and economic development requirement.

The social needs criteria are generally a "living wage" that ranges from the income necessary to support basic food, shelter, and clothing requirements for the worker, to coverage of cultural needs, children's education expenses, and leisure. The exact valuation of the needs with which a minimum wage would be equated is difficult to determine because of subjectivity in determination of the composition of the basic basket and whom to include in the definition of the family. The difficulty becomes even greater when putting a monetary value on the more abstract concepts. For example, the criteria in some countries require a minimum wage sufficient to ensure the "well-being" of workers and their families or a wage that guarantees a "dignified existence." Across the world, countries have struggled to define formulas to quantify these criteria for minimum wage setting (Starr 1993).

The ability to pay criterion usually refers to firm or industry constraints. This is also difficult to quantify, as demonstrated by efforts across the world. Whereas some countries have examined a subset of firm balance sheets to measure the degree to which the firms can pay higher wages, there is difficulty in aggregating these measures, and they do not account for international competition, which is beyond the control of national authorities. Also, the target beneficiaries of the minimum wage will determine which industries to consider, which is another subjective choice by the policy makers. Thus, these criteria are rarely quantified.

Equity criteria are plagued with measurement difficulties, as well. When determining a minimum, there are no strong guidelines for determining the minimum acceptable level of income in a society, what society considers "fair," and who constitutes the benchmark population.

Macrodevelopment requirements are even more difficult to quantify, since we still have little understanding of the relationship between economic outcomes—such as employment rates, inflation, economic growth—and the level of minimum wages. Understanding the desired target population for the minimum wage is also important, since that will determine the extent to which the minimum wage could affect these macro-outcomes.

As a result, governments usually consider the criteria behind needs, ability to pay, and macroeconomic issues, but a sense of equity is the final determinant. In preparation for wage deliberations, wage boards, worker and employer representatives, labor ministries, and finance ministries do the calculations. Once a figure is determined, however, it is not uncommon to weigh the figure against the general wage distribution and social norms and adjust accordingly (Starr 1993).

Indexation can be a useful criterion for the adjustment, but a poorly chosen index can create difficulties. Ideally, an exogenous factor could be used to adjust the minimum, thus eliminating the subjective decisions described previously. Many different criteria have been used, including inflation, cost-of-living estimates, productivity growth, future inflation, and changes in the wage level. The fundamental problem with indexing to inflation or cost-of-living estimates is that they are determined by factors outside the labor market, so it may not be reasonable to link wages to nonlabor factors.[1] Productivity growth and wage trends are also problematic indexes, since practitioners must determine which sector of the economy best approximates the productivity of the minimum wage population. Using the economy as a whole will likely overestimate the minimum wage adjustment, since the minimum tends to accrue to lower-wage workers. Even the productivity of the manufacturing sector is not a particularly good measure, since LAC economies, and particularly the poor, are increasingly working in the service sector. Perhaps the worst method of indexation is to use *expected* changes in indicators. If the expectation is poorly estimated, this could lead to severe under- or overadjustment that is difficult to correct later.

The strategy for minimum wage adjustments depends on the economic, political, and social specificities of each country. The frequency of minimum wage adjustments will depend on the inflation rate, general wage movements, and political objectives. While frequent adjustments allow for better alignment of the minimum with the economic and social climate than would periodic large changes, rarer adjustments may allow for self-enforcement (better knowledge of the level of the minimum) and lower administrative costs. Similar considerations prevail regarding timing of the adjustments. Time and political goodwill are necessary for successful minimum wage deliberations and implementation, but fixing a date for an adjustment will prevent erosion of the minimum as authorities await an "ideal" time (Starr 1993).

The complexity of the minimum wage is profoundly linked to the presence and capacity of both government and nongovernmental institutions. Complex wage structures are effective in OECD countries because they coexist with institutions that allow for appropriate wage setting and effective enforceability. Although multiple minimum wages are desirable to tailor "fair" wages to a particular geographic area, skill level, or productivity level, they are successful only if an equally complex system of oversight accompanies them. The Italian and German systems of multiple minimum wages allow for such complexity, since they are monitored by the unions that negotiated the contracts. The U.S. system, with state-level minimum wages, uses state inspectors to handle monitoring and enforcement. Clearly identified actors who monitor specific minimum wages are largely absent in Latin America.

Enforcement

The extent of enforcement of the minimum wage should depend on the role that the minimum plays in a particular labor market. As mentioned throughout this report, enforcement of the minimum is difficult in LAC, where the informal sector is large but the minimum is self-enforcing to a degree. Thus, authorities may not wish to be stringent regarding inspections for noncompliance, instead allowing the market and public pressure to enforce compliance. Or the authorities may choose to value employment over higher wages and thus focus on only the most egregious cases—leaving more moderate violations unchecked, particularly if they are in line with market forces.

Incentives can be created so that firms and workers set and enforce the minimum wage. Whereas this report showed that minimum wages are self-enforcing in some countries in LAC, this can be strengthened by weaving incentives for compliance into labor contracts. For example, in Australia, the minimum wage was part of a larger labor contract negotiated by the employer and worker representatives for a particular occupation in a particular state. The contract gave some benefits to firms and other benefits to workers. Violation of one stipulation of the "awards contract" led to renegotiating the whole contract and risking even greater losses.

But there are mechanisms to improve enforcement. Enforcement of the minimum can be costly, but there are means to maximize the resources that are available. First, set a high penalty and enforce it. This will raise the expected cost of noncompliance, and risk-averse firm owners will increase their compliance rates. Second, focus on those firms most likely not to comply, namely firms that are newly opened, rural, not unionized, or small. Also, focus on firms that are most likely to employ low-wage workers, such as specific industries, small firms, and rural firms. Finally, local oversight, simple reporting of violations, and rapid response will maximize the inputs of partners and make the inspectors' jobs easier.

Minimum wages are better set and enforced if many strategic partners are included in the process, but capture must be avoided. Governments often do not have the resources to inspect all labor complaints. However, employer and worker representatives, local councils, public interest groups, and nongovernmental organizations (NGOs) can aid the government by alerting inspectors to specific violations. For this to be effective, such groups need to be part of the wage-setting process as well, so that they have ownership and the desire to enforce the wages that they helped to set. However, full representation is necessary, including those who are most at risk of losing from a higher minimum wage. If only unions and employers are present, they have the potential to bargain a union wage and then impose it on the whole country, thus setting a wage that is too high for the lower end of the labor market, where union workers (and their protected jobs, in Latin America) tend not to be found. Thus, participation by representatives of the poorest and the unemployed is crucial to set a minimum wage—or alternative social policy to counteract its negative effects—that benefit their constituency.

In sum, there is no magic menu for setting, adjusting, and enforcing minimum wage criteria, so policy makers in each country must weigh the pros and cons of each approach and determine the best methodology for their country. The international experience has taught us that social norms, economic conditions, and the objective of the minimum wage differ across countries. A single set of guidelines is therefore not feasible. This requires hard work by governments to identify what works for them and to revisit these guidelines periodically to take into account changes within the country.

Note

1. For example, in the case of a natural disaster, the CPI (Consumer Price Index) will necessarily increase while wages decrease (since productive capacity has been destroyed). A minimum wage adjustment to the CPI would severely misalign the minimum wage. Once the misalignment is built into the minimum wage, it is difficult to correct once the economy returns to an equilibrium.

CHAPTER 8

Report Conclusions and Policy Considerations

This report focused on the circumstances in which the minimum wage is an effective tool for poverty reduction. It did not attempt to comprehensively cover the issue of minimum wages in LAC. The scope was limited to a description of minimum wage institutions; wage and employment effects of an increase in the minimum wage, particularly for certain demographic groups; how minimum wages affect household poverty and inequality; and the effects of the minimum wage on public expenditures. Thus, the conclusion and policy recommendations focus on the household in the short run (up to one year) and do not attempt to sort out macroeconomic implications (growth, inflation) or related labor market behaviors (job training, promotions). The issue of whether countries should have a minimum wage is not considered. Instead, the assumption is that all counties will continue their minimum wage policies, and, with a better understanding of who is affected by different levels of the minimum wage, policy makers can design social policy portfolios to fit the needs of their constituents.

Report Conclusions

Returning to the questions presented in the introduction to this report, the following main conclusions emerge.

The Minimum Wage Is Not a Powerful Tool to Decrease Household Poverty or Inequality

On average, a minimum wage high enough to create significant changes in the labor market will not benefit the poorest households. As shown for the relatively high minimum wage in Colombia, the wage benefits of a minimum wage skip over the poor and confer its benefits on the middle of the income distribution, whereas in the moderate minimum wage economy of Brazil, the poor on average experience a small decline in incomes. In the Mexican case study, where the minimum wage is relatively low and in which no unemployment effects were found, the minimum wage increases the earnings of the poorest, but not enough to lift them out of poverty.

A similar story emerges for household inequality. Whereas those households at the bottom of the income distribution may experience the largest wage gains, they also experience the largest job loss from an increase in the minimum wage, as in the case of Brazil. In countries where the minimum is targeted to the middle of the wage distribution, such as Colombia, those in the middle of the household income distribution benefit from the minimum wage, since their wages increase while poorer households absorb the job losses. In essence, this suggests a redistribution of income from the poor and newly unemployed to the poor and middle class who keep their jobs.

Even if the unemployment effects are moderated, the minimum wage alone is not enough to guarantee that covered sector employees will rise above poverty, since the minimum wage is too low in many countries. Although it is sufficient to provide for basic subsistence for an individual in most countries in LAC, it generally falls short of this mark for families in which there are household dependents.

Minimum Wages Have a Positive Effect on Wages but a Negative Effect on Employment in LAC

Across the region, the minimum wage increases average wages. In countries with lower minimum wages, the wages of the poorest are the most affected, with declining but positive effects further up the wage distribution. This results in compressed wage distribution and thus decreased wage inequality among individuals. In countries with relatively higher minimum wages, those earning near the minimum experience an increase in wages, resulting in greater inequality relative to the poorest.

However, unemployment effects are also greatest for the lower part of the wage distribution. The unemployment effect is less uniformly noted across the Region. Similar to the OECD data, some countries show negative employment effects, whereas others show no effects. Notably, unemployment effects are larger in higher minimum wage countries and absent in very low minimum wage countries.

The minimum wage increases the wages of all, but creates unemployment for the most vulnerable groups in the labor market. Young, low-skilled, and informal sector workers are overrepresented among the minimum wage population in low minimum wage countries. An increase in the minimum wage does not disproportionately benefit these groups, as wage gains are experienced by all demographic groups (with mixed results for the informal sector). However, these more vulnerable groups bear the brunt of the unemployment effects. The net effect of an increase in the minimum wage, then, is a redistribution of income from young, low-skilled, or female workers (because of job loss) to prime-aged, skilled, or male workers who keep their jobs.

Contrary to OECD Countries, the Minimum Wage in Latin America Has Low Coverage and Low Enforcement, but a Large Impact

Since 30–70 percent of the labor force is in the informal sector, a potentially large portion of the labor force is not covered by minimum wage laws. In practice, an even smaller portion is covered, since partial enforcement of minimum wage laws is common. This may be due to a shortage of resources for labor inspections, but in some countries, it is the result of very complex minimum wage systems that are difficult to monitor. Poor information dissemination about the hundreds of minimum wages in some countries limits the public's ability to identify infractions and thus report them.

Despite low coverage and low enforcement, the minimum wage may have a larger impact than expected for two reasons. First, examination of wage distributions shows distinct clustering around the minimum wage and multiples of the minimum wage in both the formal and informal sectors. These so-called spikes and cliffs in the wage distribution indicate that wages are bunched around these values.

Second, the minimum wage is used as a numeraire. Wages are bargained relative to the minimum wage in both the formal and informal sectors; this is not due to legal statutes, but to a social convention of fairness by workers and employers, and possibly a spillover from hyperinflationary periods when an often adjusted benchmark was required for wage setting. This results in minimum wage effects in the informal sector and numeraire effects throughout the wage distribution.

The minimum wage is more binding in the informal sector than the formal. The clustering of wages around the minimum wage is greater in the informal than the formal sector. This may be due to use of the minimum wage by informal sector employers as a proxy for a "fair wage." Alternatively, since low-wage workers tend to earn the minimum wage, the observed spikes in the wage distribution may be due to a greater number of informal sector workers relative to formal sector workers, earning wages in the range of the minimum wage. Thus, there are more people to cluster around the minimum wage in the informal sector than the formal.

The Minimum Wage Is Burdensome to the Fiscal Deficit in LAC

In LAC, social expenditures are tied to the minimum wage, so any increase in the minimum wage also has large effects on the public deficit. The largest expenditure category affected in many countries is the pension system, but other benefits, ranging from salary bonuses to job training stipends to "shock benefits" (death in the family, birth, marriage, and so forth), are denominated in minimum wages. Eligibility for social programs is also tied to the minimum wage in many countries, so an increase in the minimum will also increase beneficiaries of social programs.

However, the public sector is a big employer in some countries, so even if the minimum wage is delinked from social programs, it will still create a cost to the government. Although public sector employee salaries are not subject to the official minimum wage in many countries, some type of minimum wage level does exist. Thus, increases in the minimum wage will increase government expenditures, particularly at local levels where wages are lower and thus more subject to the minimum wage. However, the extent of the increase is largely due to the size of the minimum wage and of the public sector. In countries with a low minimum wage, the effects are barely felt, while in countries with a large public sector, the effects are very strong.

The minimum wage is not a good proxy for subsistence needs. It is insufficient to provide for family needs in half of the countries in LAC. Thus, a poverty measure is more appropriate for targeting social protection programs and for acting as a numeraire for social protection payments. Or, as in Chile, another "nonwage" minimum can be set for indexing social protection programs.

High Minimum Wage Levels Do Not Necessarily Benefit the Poorest

The three case studies in this report—Colombia, Brazil, and Mexico—have relatively high, medium, and low minimum wages in PPP-adjusted currency.

They also show that the benefits of the minimum wage accrue to those who are earning near the minimum wage. If the minimum wage is too high, it will pass over the poorest and instead benefit those whose market wages are close to it. The unemployment effects tend to fall on the poorest, though, leading to a very regressive tax on the poor.

Considerations for Policy Debates

The indirect effects of a minimum wage make it an imperfect tool for income redistribution. Also, there is spillover, so that the net benefits may accrue (more) to the middle class rather than the working poor. Rather, direct redistribution is more effective for targeting beneficiaries and limiting the perverse labor supply incentives effects that can arise from the market-based program. Of course, such tax-and-spend policies are difficult to carry out, since taxes are politically undesirable, the identification of beneficiaries is difficult, and creating and monitoring institutions that distribute money would be challenging.

The minimum wage has its benefits, though, and can be used as a redistributive tool if it is accompanied by a safety net for the unemployed. The unemployment effects of the minimum wage counterbalance the desired redistributive effects, so income is redistributed from those who lose their jobs to those who keep their jobs. To decrease the regressivity of the scheme, support for the unemployed is required, funded by workers themselves through unemployment insurance schemes that redistribute income from all those who are working to those who lose their jobs.[1] Of course, this scheme misses the informal sector workers, so social assistance schemes may also be necessary.

If an unemployment insurance scheme exists, the minimum wage may be a good alternative for income redistribution. An unemployment insurance–enhanced minimum wage system is superior to a direct transfer for three principal reasons. First, a minimum wage is self-targeted, so the complicated process of identifying the target group is eliminated. Second, it is self-financing, so the market, rather than taxes and public spending, provides the social welfare benefits. Tax collection and the allocation of public funds are politically and practically difficult. General taxes are not well received by taxpayers, even if they are earmarked for social programs. A minimum wage system indirectly imposes a tax, which is interpreted as a job loss resulting from bad luck, rather than a tax policy with social ends. The allocation of public funds is also difficult because it is associated with *asistencialismo* and *clientelismo*, both unsavory practices. However, if the market redistributes, these practices are not an issue.

Third, it gives individuals the incentive to work rather than to remain without income and live off the system. One of the greatest arguments against direct transfers is the disincentive to hold a job. However, the minimum wage provides social assistance *only if the individual is employed.* Furthermore, since all workers prefer to earn higher wages, and minimum wages help working poor above the minimum wage as well, there is no disincentive to work longer or seek promotions; the individual will not lose from doing well in the labor market.

Regardless of the social justice objectives or the nature of the social policy portfolio, existing minimum wage systems can be improved as follows:

Create a support to unemployment that redistributes income from all workers (not just the working poor) to those who lose their jobs.

Fewer and simpler is better. The minimum wage is a difficult tool for pegging informal sector wages and for enforcing if it is not well defined. The international evidence tells us that a minimum wage should be as complex as possible to accurately provide wage floors that may differ by region, profession, skill level, and so forth. However, the more tailored the minimum wage is to specific populations, the less it is used by the general population. Thus, the policy maker needs to balance the specificity of the minimum wage with the ability of the state and society to use the minimum.

Clear criteria. A complex minimum wage system makes it difficult for workers to understand if they are being paid a legal wage and for using the minimum wage as a benchmark. The importance of the minimum wage in the informal sector throughout the region points to the self-enforcement nature of the minimum wage and the need for simple, well-known minimum wage levels. By making clear the value of the minimum and the criteria for selecting the level at which it is set, self-enforcement becomes more possible.

An inclusive system for wage setting is preferred, but all parties must be represented. The system of a government–trade union–employer group wage-setting process is not effective, since they collapse into a union-employer arrangement. Whereas the government should represent the unemployed, government in reality represents all actors in society. Thus, a balance should be found between representation of the unemployed and representation of those who are most hurt by the minimum, namely the unemployed, youth, low-skilled, and women. This is not a simple process, but its long-run effects have proven successful in OECD countries.

The minimum wage must be delinked from other public sector expenditure. The minimum wage is not a good proxy for a minimum subsistence level, so there is no reason to tie it to other social programs. This link does not allow for the minimum wage to be set according to market conditions because it is tied up in other public issues. Thus, social programs are best tied to another poverty measure, while the minimum wage is allowed to fluctuate according to market characteristics and complementary social programs are present to compensate for the negative employment effects.

Experimentation. The best level of the minimum depends on (a) the policy objectives of the government in setting a minimum, (b) other institutions in the country that can complement or substitute for the effects of the minimum, (c) labor market conditions (demand elasticities, supply elasticities, elasticity of substitution between skilled and less skilled workers, enforcement mechanisms, level of external and internal competition in the product markets, for example), and (d) the macroeconomic situation. The best level for the minimum wage cannot be identified by a formula; instead, it is subject to trial and error, with a strong impact evaluation agenda.

Overall, the minimum wage is a social justice tool that is important in LAC's social policy portfolio, and it possesses characteristics that make it a desirable policy. The challenge is to set the minimum wage to maximize social justice objectives while minimizing the perverse effects of the minimum wage. Other social programs can offset the latter, thus improving the social outcomes of minimum wage policies in LAC.

Note

1. Individual savings accounts would not have the desired effect, since there is no income pooling.

References

Abowd, John, Francis Kramarz, and David Margoliz. 1999. "Minimum Wages and Employment in France and the United States." NBER Working Paper 6996, National Bureau of Economic Research, Cambridge.

Agenor, Pierre-Richard, and Joshua Aizenman. 1999. "Macroeconomic Adjustment with Segmented Labor Markets." *Journal of Development Economics* 58: 277–96.

Anderson, T., and C. Hsiao. 1981. "Estimation of Dynamic Models with Error Components." *Journal of the American Statistical Association* 76: 598–606.

Angel-Urdinola, Diego, and Quentin Wodon. 2003. "The Impact on Inequality of Raising the Minimum Wage: Gap-Narrowing and Reranking Effects." Georgetown University, Washington, DC.

Arango, Carlos, and William F. Maloney. 2000. "Reform and Income Insecurity in Argentina and Mexico." Draft. World Bank, Washington, DC.

Arango, Carlos, and Angelica Pachon. 2003. "Distributive Effects of Minimum Wages on Household Incomes: Colombia 1997–2002." Banco de la República, Bogotá, Colombia.

Arellano, M., and S. Bond. 1991. "Some Tests of Specification for Panel Data: Monte Carlo Evidence and an Application to Employment Equations." *Review of Economic Studies* 58: 277–97.

Arias, Omar. 1999. "Marginalization of Men in Argentina: Evidence from Changes in Wage Distributions." World Bank, Washington, DC.

Becker, Gary. 1976. "Altruism, Egoism, and Genetic Fitness: Economics and Sociobiology." *Journal of Economic Literature* 14(3): 817–26.

Bell, Linda. 1997. "The Impact of Minimum Wages in Mexico and Colombia." *Journal of Labor Economics* (July): S102–35.

Bravo, David, and Joaquin Vial. 1997. "La Fijación del salario mínimo en Chile: elementos para una discusión." *Colección Estudios CIEPLAN* #45.

Brown, Charlie. 1999. "Minimum Wages, Employment and the Distribution of Income." In *The Handbook of Labor Economics*, Volume 3b, ed. O. Ashenfelter and D. Card, 2101–63.

Burkhauser, Richard V., Kenneth A. Couch, and David C. Wittenburg. 1996. "'Who Gets What' from Minimum Wage Hikes: A Re-estimation of Card and Krueger's Distributional Analysis in *Myth and Measurement: The New Economics of the Minimum Wage.*" *Industrial & Labor Relations Review* 49(3): 547–52.

Card, David, Francis Kramarz, and Thomas Lemieux. 1999. "Changes in the Relative Structure of Wages and Employment: A Comparison of the United States, Canada, and France." *Canadian Journal of Economics* 32(4): 843–77.

Card, David, and Alan Krueger. 1994. "Minimum Wages and Employment: A Case Study of the Fast-Food Industry in New Jersey and Pennsylvania." *American Economic Review* (September): 772–93.

———. 1995. *Myth and Measurement: The New Economics of the Minimum Wage.* Princeton, NJ: Princeton University Press.

Carneiro, Francisco. 2000. "The Impact of Minimum Wages on Wages, Employment, and Informality in Brazil." Unpublished.

Carneiro, Francisco Galrao. 2002. "An Overview of the Effects of the Minimum Wages on the Brazilian Labor Market." In *Brazil Jobs Report*, Volume II, Report No. 24408-BR, ed. Indermit Gill, Ricardo Paes de Barros, and Andreas Blom, 131–63. Washington, DC: World Bank.

Carneiro, Francisco, and João Ricardo Faria. 1997. "Causality between the Minimum Wage and Other Wages."*Applied Economics Letters* (4), 507–10.

Castellanos, Sara G., Rodrigo Garcia-Verdu, and David Kaplan. 2004. "Nominal Wage Rigidities in Mexico: Evidence from Social Security Records." *Journal of Development Economics* 75(2): 507–33.

Corseuil, C., and Francisco Carneiro. 2001. "Os impactos do salário mínimo sobre emprego e salários no Brasil: evidências a partir de dados Longitudinais e Series Temporais." Texto para Discussão No. 849, IPEA, Rio de Janeiro.

Corseuil, Carlos Henrique, and Luciana M. S. Servo. 2002. "Salario mínimo e Bem-Estar Social no Brasil: uma resenha da literatura." Texto para Discussão No. 880, IPEA, Rio de Janeiro.

Cunningham, Wendy. 2002. "The Poverty Implications of Minimum Wages in Developing Countries." In *Brazil Jobs Report*, Volume II, Report No. 24408-BR, ed. Indermit Gill, Ricardo Paes de Barros, and Andreas Blom, 164–88. Washington, DC: World Bank.

Cunningham, Wendy, and William F. Maloney. 2002. "Heterogeneity in the Mexican Micro-enterprise Sector." *Economic Development and Cultural Change* 50(1): 31–156.

Cunningham, Wendy, and Mauricio Santamaria. 2003. "The Labor Market as a Source of Income Inequality." World Bank, Washington, DC.

Cunningham, Wendy, and Lucas Siga. 2006. "Wage and Employment Effects of Minimum Wages on Vulnerable Groups in the Labor Market: Brazil and Mexico." World Bank/LCSHS, Washington, DC.

Currie, Janet, and Bruce Fallick. 1996. "The Minimum Wage and the Employment of Youth Evidence from the NLSY." *The Journal of Human Resources* 31(20): 404–28.

Devarajan, Shantayanan, Hafez Ghanem, and Karen Theirfelder. 1997. "Economic Reform and Labor Unions: A General-Equilibrium Analysis Applied to Bangladesh and Indonesia." *World Bank Economic Review* 11(1): 145–70.

DiNardo, J., N. Fortin, and T. Lemieux. 1996. "Labor Market Institutions and the Distribution of Wages 1973–1992: A Semiparametric Approach." *Econometrica* (September): 1001–44.

DiNardo, John, and Justin L. Tobias. 2001. "Nonparametric Density and Regression Estimation." *Journal of Economic Perspectives* 15(4): 11–28.

Fajnzylber, Pablo. 2002. "Minimum Wage Effects throughout the Wage Distribution: Evidence from Brazil's Formal and Informal Sectors." Universidade Federal de Minas Gerais, Department of Economics and CEDE-PLAR. Belo Horizante, Brazil.

Fajnzylber, Pablo, Daniel Lederman, and Norman Loayza. 1998. *Determinants of Crime Rates in Latin America and the World*. Washington, DC: World Bank.

Ferreira, F., P. Lanjouw, and M. Neri. 2000. "A new poverty profile for Brazil using PPV, PNAD, and census data." Texto para Discussão No. 418. Pontificia Universidade Catolica-Rio, Department of Economics, Rio de Janeiro.

Fiszbein, Ariel. 1992. "Do Workers in the Informal Sector Benefit from Cuts in the Minimum Wage?" Working Paper Series 826, World Bank, Washington, DC.

Foguel, Miguel Nathan. 1997. "Uma Análise dos efeitos do salario mínimo sobre o mercado de trabalho no Brasil." Master's thesis, Pontificia Universidade Catolica-Rio, Rio de Janeiro.

Foguel, Miguel, Carlos Henrique Corseuil, Ricardo Paes de Barros, and Phillippe Leite. 2000. "Uma Avaliacão dos impactos do salario mínimo sobre o nivel de pobreza Metropolitana no Brasil." Texto para Discussão No. 739, IPEA, Rio de Janeiro.

Foguel, Miguel, Lauro Ramos, and Francisco Carneiro. 2001. "The Impact of the Minimum Wage on Labor Market, Poverty, and Fiscal Budget in Brazil." Texto para Discussão No. 839, IPEA, Rio de Janeiro.

Garza Cantú, Vidal, and Fernando Bazaldúa. 2002. "La Dinámica Macroeconómica de los Salarios Mínimos en el Empleo de México: Un Análisis Empírico 1983–2000." In Comisión Nacional de los Salarios Mínimos (eds.) Comisión Consultiva para la Modernización del Sistema de los Salario Mínimos: Estudios y Ponencias (STPS: Mexico).

Geldstein, Rosa. 2000. "Non-Labor Market Coping Strategies in Argentina." LCSPG/World Bank, Washington, DC.

Ghellab, Y. 1998. "Minimum Wage and Youth Unemployment." ILO Employment and Training Papers. International Labour Organization, Geneva.

Gindling, T. H., and Katherine Terrell. 2005. "The Effect of Minimum Wages on Actual Wages in Formal and Informal Sectors in Costa Rica." World Development 33(11): 1905.

Gonzaga, Gustavo, and João Scandiuzzi. 1998. "How Does Government Wage Policy Affect Wage Bargaining in Brazil?" Revista Econometria 18(1): 1–31.

Gorman, Linda. "Minimum Wages." The Concise Encyclopedia of Economics. http://www.econlib.org/library/Enc/MinimumWages.html. Accessed January 2007.

Grossman, J. 1983. "The Impact of Minimum Wage on Other Wages." Journal of Human Resources (Summer): 359–78.

Guzman, Rolando, Madalena Lizardo, and Dayana Lora. 2003. "Minimum Wage and Public Finance in Selected Latin American Countries: The Cases of Panama, Brazil, Colombia, Mexico, and the Dominican Republic." World Bank/LCSHS, Washington, DC.

Haddad, Lawrence, John Hoddinott, and Harold Alderman. 1997. Intrahousehold Resource Allocation in Developing Countries. Baltimore: Johns Hopkins University Press.

Harris, J. R., and M. P. Todaro. 1970. "Migration, Unemployment, and Development: A Two Sector Analysis." American Economic Review 60(1): 126–42.

Heckman, James, and Carmen Pagés. 2004. Law and Employment: Lessons from Latin America and the Caribbean. Chicago: University of Chicago Press.

Horrigan, M., and R. Mincy. 1993. "Minimum Wage and Earnings and Income Inequality." In *Uneven Tides: Rising Inequality in America*, ed. S. Danziger and P. Gottschalk, 251–75. Russell Sage Foundation: New York.

IDB (Inter-American Development Bank). 2000. *Facing Up to Inequality.* Washington, DC: Inter-American Development Bank.

IPEA (Instituto de Pesquisa Económica Aplicada). 2000a. *Impactos do salario mínimo sobre a folha de pagamentos das tres esferas de governo.* Rio de Janeiro.

————. 2000b. *Salario minimo no Brasil: impactos sobre as contas da previdencia social.* Rio de Janiero.

————. 2000c. *Uma Analise da eficacia das politicas publicas de trábalo e renda no combate a probreza no Brasil.* Rio de Janiero.

Katz, Lawrence, and Alan Krueger. 1992. "The Effect of the Minimum Wage on the Fast-Food Industry." *Industrial and Labor Relations Review* (October): 6–21.

Kristensen, Nicolai, and Wendy Cunningham. 2006. "Do Minimum Wages in Latin America and the Caribbean Matter: Evidence from 19 Countries." Policy Research Working Paper 3870, World Bank, Washington, DC.

Lemos, Sara. 2002a. "Robust Quantification of Minimum Wage Effects on Wages and Employment Using a New Data Set—a Menu of Minimum Wage Variables." University College, London.

Loxley, John, and Vali Jamal. 1999. "Structural Adjustment and Agriculture in Guyana: From Crisis to Recovery." ILO Working Paper 143, International Labour Office, Geneva.

Lustig, N., and D. McLeod. 1996. "Minimum Wages and Poverty in Developing Countries: Some Empirical Evidence." Brookings Discussion Papers in International Economics DP No. 125. Brookings Institution, Washington, DC.

Machin, Stephen, and Alan Manning. 1994. "The Effects of Minimum Wages on Wage Dispersion and Employment: Evidence from the U.K. Wage Councils." *Industrial and Labor Relations Review* (January): 319–29.

————. 1996. "Employment and the Introduction of a Minimum Wage in Britain." *Economic Journal* (106): 667–76.

Maloney, W. F. 1999. "Does Informality Imply Segmentation in Urban Labor Markets? Evidence from Sectoral Transitions in Mexico." *World Bank Economic Review* 13: 275–302.

————. 2003. "Informality Revisited." Policy Research Working Paper 2965, World Bank, Washington, DC.

Maloney, W. F., and J. Nunez. 2004. "Measuring the Impact of Minimum Wages, Evidence from Latin America." In *Law and Employment: Lessons from Latin America and the Caribbean*, ed. James Heckman and Carmen Pages, 109–30. Chicago: University of Chicago Press, National Bureau of Economic Research.

May, Ernesto, ed. 1993. *Poverty in Colombia*. Washington, DC: World Bank.

Mazumdar, D. 1983. "Segmented Labor Markets in LDCs." *American Economic Review* (73): 254–9.

Mincer, Jacob. 1962. "Labor Force Participation of Married Women." In *Aspects of Labor Economics*, ed. H. Greg Lewis, 63–97. Universities NBER Conference Series No. 14. Princeton, NJ: Princeton University Press.

Montenegro, Claudio. 2003. "Unemployment, Job Security, and Minimum Wages in Chile: 1960–2001." Human Development Sector Unit, Background Paper 5, World Bank, Washington, DC.

Morley, Samuel. 1992. "Structural Adjustment and the Determinants of Poverty in Latin America." Vanderbilt University, Department of Economics and Business Administration, Working Paper No. 92, Nashville, TN.

Neri, Marcelo, Gustavo Gonzaga, and Jose Marcio Camargo. 2000. "Efeitos Informais do Salario Minimo e Pobreza." Texto Para Discussão No. 724, IPEA, Rio de Janeiro.

Neumark, David, Wendy Cunningham, and Lucas Siga. 2006. "The Effects of the Minimum Wage in Brazil on the Distribution of Family Incomes: 1996–2001." *Journal of Development Economics* (80): 136–59.

Neumark, David, Mark Schweitzer, and William Wascher. 2000. "The Effects of Minimum Wages Throughout the Wage Distribution." NBER Working Paper 7519, National Bureau of Economic Research, Cambridge, MA.

Neumark, David, and William Wascher. 1997. "Do Minimum Wages Fight Poverty?" NBER Working Paper 6127, National Bureau of Economic Research, Cambridge, MA.

———. 1998. "The Effects of Minimum Wages on the Distribution of Family Incomes: A Nonparametric Analysis." NBER Working Paper 6536, National Bureau of Economic Research, Cambridge, MA.

Nordlund, Willis J. 1997. *The Quest for a Living Wage: The History of the Federal Minimum Wage Program*. Westport, Connecticut: Greenwood Press.

Pagan, Adrian, and Aman Ullah. 1999. *Nonparametric Econometrics*. Cambridge: Cambridge University Press.

Ramos, Lauro, and Jose Guilherme Almeida Reis. 1995. "Salario mínimo, distribução de renda e pobreza no Brasil." *Pesquisa e Planejamento* 25 (1): 99–114.

Ridley, Jasper. 1999. *The Freemasons: A History of the World's Most Secret Society*. New York: Arcade Publishing.

Robertson, D., and J. Symons. 1992. "Some Strange Properties of Panel Data Estimators." *Journal of Applied Econometrics* 7: 175–89.

Rodrígues, Eduardo, Augusto de Souza, and Naercio Aquino Menezes Filho. 2003. "Minimum Wage and Inequality in Brazil, Mexico, and Argentina,

1981–2000: A Semi-parametric Approach." Universidade de São Paulo/ World Bank, São Paulo.

Ruiz, Maria. 2001. "La Reforma laboral en América Latina: un análisis comparado." International Labour Office, Geneva.

Ruprah, Inder, and Luis Marcano. 1998. "Poverty Alleviation in Venezuela: Whom to Target and How Not to Adjust in a Crisis." Inter-American Development Bank, Regional Operations Department 3, Washington, DC.

Soares, Sergei Suarez. 2002. "O Impacto distributivo do salario mínimo: a distribução individual dos rendimentos do trabalho." Texto para Discussão No. 873, IPEA, Rio de Janeiro.

Starr, Gerald. 1993. *Minimum Wage Fixing: An International Review of Practices and Problems.* Geneva: International Labour Office.

Stiglitz, Joseph E. 1984. "Alternative Theories of Wage Determination and Unemployment in LDCs: The Labor Turnover Model." *Quarterly Journal of Economics* 88: 194–227.

Trinder, Chris. 1984. "Issues from Recent Minimum Wage Research." In *Policies against Low Pay: An International Perspective,* ed. Frank Field. London: Policy Studies Institute.

Webb, Sidney. 1912. "The Economic Theory of a Legal Minimum Wage." *Journal of Political Economy* 20 (10): 973–98.

World Bank. 1995. *World Development Report.* Washington, DC: World Bank.

———. 1999. *Poverty and Social Development in Peru, 1994–97.* Washington, DC: World Bank.

———. 2000. *Panama Poverty Assessment: Priorities and Strategies for Poverty Reduction.* Washington, DC: World Bank.

———. 2001a. *Honduras Poverty Diagnostic 2000.* Report No. 20531-HO. Washington, DC: World Bank.

———. 2001b. *Maintaining Social Equity in a Changing Economy.* Report No. 21262. Washington, DC: World Bank.

———. 2001c. *Nicaragua – Poverty Assessment: Challenges and Opportunities for Poverty Reduction.* Report No. 20488. Washington, DC: World Bank.

———. 2002. *Guatemala: Livelihoods, Labor Markets, and Rural Poverty.* Washington, DC: World Bank.

Zavodny, Madeline. 2000. "The Effect of the Minimum Wage on Employment and Hours." *Labour Economics* 7 (6): 729–50.

Research Methodologies

The background papers prepared for this report use the newest methodologies for measuring the impact of policy variables. Various methodologies are employed for each country to verify that the findings are robust.

(i) Econometric Methodology for Measuring the Impact of Minimum Wages on Wages, Employment and Poverty: Cases: Brazil, Colombia, and Mexico (Siga and Cunningham 2006)

Neumark, Schweitzer, and Wascher (2000) use rotating panel data from the United States to test the impact of a rise in the minimum wage on wages and the probability of becoming unemployed, and for numeraire effects in both. Subsequent work extended the exercise to look at the impact on household poverty. The methodology was employed by Maloney and Nuñez for Colombia (2004) for wages and employment; we repeat the exercise for Brazil and Mexico and in addition, estimate the impact on household income. Each country offers a panel from which household incomes can be constructed and followed across time.

Estimation methodology. The panel nature of the data permits identification of the impact of minimum wage changes on wages, employment, and household earnings. The determinants of the percentage change in the real hourly wage worker i receives (dw), the probability of becoming unemployed (prob $z = 1$), or change in the real household income (dh) across the period are identified as:

$$
\begin{aligned}
dw_i,\ prob(z = 1),\ dh = &\sum_j \beta_j R\left(w_{i1}, mw_1\right)_j \left[\frac{mw_2 - mw_1}{mw_1}\right] \\
&+ \sum_j \gamma_j R\left(w_{i1}, mw_1\right)_j + \sum_j \phi_j R\left(w_{i1}, mw_1\right)_j \left[\frac{w_{i1}}{mw_1}\right] \\
&+ \delta X_{i1} + \lambda T_i + \pi A_i + \varepsilon_i
\end{aligned}
\tag{1}
$$

where mw is the real minimum wage, respectively, in the two periods.

Although it is common to examine the impact of the minimum wage on wages and employment at the minimum wage, the kernel density plots suggest that there are numeraire effects throughout the distribution. If we are interested in the total effect of the mw on distribution and employment, we need to look for these effects as well. Further, there may be general equilibrium effects at higher wage levels through changes in relative demand. For these reasons, we create a vector of j dummy variables, R, that locate individual i's wage in the real hourly wage distribution in year 1 at fractions and multiples of the minimum wage. This allows us to see the impact of a change of minimum wage, not only on those earning one minimum wage, but also those earning, for example, two or three times the minimum wage.

The first term on the right-hand side of the equation captures this effect of a change in the minimum wage on different regions of the wage distribution. The second term permits the level of wage growth, independent of minimum wage effects, to change by each cohort in the wage distribution. The third term induces more flexibility in the function, allowing the estimation of the implicit spline specification without constraining the lines to join at the knot points.

Finally, X is a vector with the individual characteristics such as gender, age, education, and so forth; T and A are a set of quarterly and regional dummy variables that capture the dependence of observations of the same period (including seasonal effects) and region, respectively.

Previous papers find that low-income families receive a short-run benefit when the minimum wage increases but are negatively affected over the longer term (Neumark and Wascher 1997; Neumark, Schweitzer, and Wascher 2000). This is because short-run adjustments are made through prices and long-run adjustments through quantities: firms must follow the law at first, but then, if necessary, they fire workers. For this reason, a lagged minimum wage $(MW_1 - MW_0)/MW_0$ is introduced.

Data. The data used in the exercise were the Encuesta Nacional de Empleo Urbano (ENEU—National Urban Employment Survey), 1988–1999, for Mexico, and the Pesquisa Mensual de Emprego (PME—Monthly Employment Survey), 1996–2001 for Brazil. Whereas wages tend to adjust quickly, employment adjustments take longer. Thus, a one-year lag was permitted between the first and second observation to allow for the long-term wage and employment effect to occur.

(ii) **Econometric Methodology for Measuring the Impact of Minimum Wages on Wages, Employment, and Poverty: Brazil (Neumark, Cunningham, and Siga 2006)**

This paper uses cross-section time series data to measure the correlation between fluctuations in the minimum wage and in the mean wage at each wage decile. These data require a minimum wage variable that captures both time series variation in the level of the minimum wage and cross-sectional variation in the "bite" of the minimum.

Data. The PME for May 1996–August 2001 was used. While most of the analysis uses this period, one exercise includes one-year lags, thus using data back to May 1995. This period largely avoids the hyperinflationary period of the late 1980s and early 1990s and the wage indexing that occurred through much of the 1990s. The survey covers six metropolitan areas in Brazil: São Paulo, Rio de Janeiro, Pôrto Alegre, Pernambuco, Recife, and Belo Horizonte. Only households with positive earnings and no missing income reported are included, for a sample size of 1,417,120 families and 2,380,662 employed individuals.

Identification of the minimum wage proxy. The first step was to identify the variable that would proxy changes in the minimum wage. The percentage below variable (for any metropolitan area–month cell, the percentage of individuals three months earlier whose wages were below the t + 3 mw) was defined as

$$PB_{jt} = P(w_{ijt-3} < mw_t) * 100$$

For i = individual, j = metropolitan area, and t = month, w = wage, mw = minimum wage, and P = probability that the condition holds. To test if PB_{jt} is a good measure of the treatment effect, the following model was estimated (GLS with AR1 process) by centile:

$$w_{jt}^c = \alpha + \beta PB_{jt} + C_{j\gamma} + M_t \delta + \varepsilon_{jt} \qquad (2)$$

where w^c is the cth centile of the real wage distribution in metropolitan area j in month t, C is a vector of dummy variables for the metropolitan area, and M is a set of dummy variables for each month. PB is the "percentage below" the minimum.

Distributional effects on family income. The following equation was estimated for 10 centiles of the household income distribution:

$$FI_{jt}^c = \alpha + \Sigma_k^K \beta_k PB_{jt-3} + C_{j\gamma} + \delta M_t + \varepsilon_{jt} \qquad (3)$$

Where FI = c^{th} centile of the distribution of per capita family income, and the other variables are as defined above. The expectation is that increases in the mw in lower-wage metropolitan areas, resulting in larger increases in the percentage below, will generate larger changes in the lower centiles of the distribution of family income in low-wage areas.

Labor supply effects. To understand why the poverty levels and inequality measures move as they do, labor supply effects for the various centiles are also examined. A simple OLS is estimated for hours worked and employment of household heads, and again for nonhousehold heads:

$$E_{jt}, H_{jt} = \alpha + \Sigma_k^K \beta_k PB_{jt-3} + C_{j\gamma} + \delta M_t + \varepsilon_{jt} \qquad (4)$$

Where E is a dummy for employment and H measures monthly hours worked. The variable of interest is again the β'. The regression is estimated separately for the household head and household dependents.

(iii) Econometric Methodology for Measuring the Impact of Minimum Wages on Wages, Employment, and Poverty: Cases: Colombia (Arango and Pachón 2003)

This paper uses a methodology similar to that used in (ii), but unlike in Brazil, the regional variation could not be exploited in Colombia, since a substantial portion of the population earned at or below the minimum wage across the country. Instead, a longer time series is used, where the time variation allows for identification of correlations between the minimum wage and the household per capita income (and wages, employment, and hours of workers) for various income centiles.

Minimum wage proxies. Two variables are used to identify the minimum wage: the "fraction below" variable (FB), which is the proportion of the population between the old and new minimum wage (the portion that "should" be swept up by the new minimum), and a standard real minimum wage to median income ratio to test the robustness of our estimates (MB).

Analogous to taxation, the fraction will measure changes in the base, whereas the minimum median ratio will measure changes in the level.

Data. The Encuesta Nacional de Hogares (ENH) 1984–2001 is used. Families that report zero income are dropped, as are those families where a working individual does not report a positive income (unless that person declares himself or herself as an unpaid worker).

Exercise 1: labor supply effects. A dynamic panel model is estimated:

$$y_j = \alpha + \beta_1 MB_{jt} + \beta_2 MB_{jt-1/4} + \beta_3 MB_{jt-1/2} + \beta_4 MB_{jt-1} + \gamma_x' X_j + \gamma_z' Z_j$$

$$+ \gamma_y' D_y + \gamma_q' D_q + \gamma_{yq}' D_{yq} + \gamma_c' D_c + \varepsilon_j \tag{5}$$

where y_j is an outcome variable for individual j, X_j is a set of human capital variables of individual j, Z_j is a set of other individual characteristics, D_y, D_q, D_c, and D_{yc} are year, quarter, city, and interacted year-city dummies. A probit is used to estimate the effect of the minimum wage on the probability of household heads being employed, and a Tobit is used to estimate the hours worked of the head. Similarly, a Tobit is used to estimate the hours worked of nonhousehold heads, where j is a family (rather than individual) indicator, X_j are household human capital variables (maximum education level in household, maximum age of the household members participating in the labor force, the proportion of women among family members, the proportion of self-employed among working members of the labor force, and the proportion of children in the household), and Z_j are other household control variables. A binomial model is used to estimate unemployment and labor force participation of nonhousehold heads.

Exercise 2: wage and household income effects. A dynamic panel model is estimated for each (of 10) percentile of the wage (household per capita income) distribution. For both proxies of the minimum wage bite (MB), the model is estimated:

$$y_{jt}^c = \alpha + \eta y_{jt-1}^c + \beta MB_{jt} + \mu_j + \lambda_t + \varepsilon_{jt} \tag{6}$$

where y_{jt}^c is the cth centile of the distribution of wages (per capita family incomes) in city j in year t, MB_{jt} is a proxy of the minimum wage bite for each city-quarter pair, μ_j is a city unobservable effect and λ_t is a time-specific effect, invariant across cities.[1] The estimate for β measures the short-run effect, while $\beta/(1-\eta)$ measures the long-run effect.

Equation (6) is estimated following Anderson and Hsiao (1982) differences estimator but, since the panels are characterized by small n

(seven cities) and quite large T (16 observations), the strategy suggested by Robertson and Symons (1992) is followed. First panel unit roots are tested for both the dependent and the independent variables.[2] The null of unit root was not rejected for any of the variables used in the estimation. In such cases, Robert et al. show that the instrumental variables estimator of Arellano and Bond (1991) does not work well, since lags of the dependent variable in levels will not be correlated with the lags of the dependent variable in differences. They then suggest using lags of the exogenous variables in differences as instruments, so lags of the minimum wage bite proxies defined above are used. By estimating (6) in differences, city effects are eliminated but not the time effect, so time dummies are added to the specification.

Exercise 3: distributive effects. Since each centile in exercise 2 is estimated separately, it is not possible to determine whether the estimated coefficients (namely the β for each centile) are statistically different from each other, thus the statistical significance of the distributive effects of the minimum wage cannot be estimated. To gauge this, a difference-in-differences estimator is used, where the difference between each percentile and the median percentile for both family per capita incomes and individual labor incomes is used. Following equation (6) and subtracting y_{jt}^c from $y_{jt}^{0.5}$ for any c^{th} centile of the income distribution we get:

$$y_{jt}^{0.5} - y_{jt}^c = \alpha_d + \eta^m y_{jt-1}^m - \eta^c y_{jt-1}^c$$
$$+ (\beta^m - \beta^c)MB_{jt} + \varepsilon_{jt}^m - \varepsilon_{jt}^c \tag{7}$$

Equation (7) is estimated using Anderson and Hsiao (1982) and Robertson and Symons (1992), using as instruments for the lagged differences in the percentile incomes $\Delta y_{ji-1}^{0.5}$ and Δy_{ji-1}^c with lagged differences in our proxies for the minimum wage bite FB and MB.

(iv) **Econometric Methodology for Measuring the Impact of Minimum Wages on the Wage Distribution Cases: Argentina, Brazil, and Mexico (Rodriguez and Filho 2003)**

The methodology of this work follows that proposed by DiNardo, Fortin, and Lemieux (1996). This approach is quite similar to the Oaxaca decomposition. However, instead of working with means, the decomposition here is based on the distribution of wages. It is based on simple counterfactual distributions, such as "What would have been the density of wages in 1988 if the characteristics of workers had been the same as those observed in 1981?"

The difference between the density of wages in 1988 and the counterfactual density associated with the minimum wage will give us the potential effect this factor would have on the wage distribution. The difference between the counterfactual density of the minimum and the counterfactual associated with the characteristics of workers, in turn, would give us the potential effect of these characteristics already discounting the effects of the minimum wage. The difference between the density of the last factor considered and the density for 1981 would give us the unexplained changes. And naturally, the sum of all the effects must equal the difference between the densities for 1988 and 1981. Mathematically, we have that

$$f_{88}(w) - f_{81}(w) = \{f_{88}(w) - f_{SM}(w)\} + \{f_{SM}(w) - f_z(w)\} + \{f_z(w) - f_{81}(w)\} \quad (8)$$

where $f_{SM}(w)$ is the counterfactual density associated with the minimum wage and $f_z(w)$ is that associated with the other individual characteristics.

To estimate the density of monthly wages, the kernel method (DiNardo and Tobias 2001) is used, adapted to include sample weights for each observation. For the counterfactual densities, the kernel method is also used, but with the careful choice of a reweighter.

Part 1: kernel estimates. The kernel estimator of a probability density function, $f(w)$, is obtained from the following formula—adapted to include the sample weights for each observation:

$$\hat{f}(w) = \sum_{i \in S} \frac{\theta_i}{b} \cdot K\left(\frac{w - W_i}{b}\right) \quad (9)$$

where θ_i is the sample weight of observation i (which is the weight of each point of Brazil's PNAD sample and equals 1 in Argentina's and Mexico's samples), S is the set of indexes of the observations of the sample, b is the smoothing parameter (bandwidth), $K(.)$ is the kernel function, and W_i are the sample wages.

The kernel function used is the Gaussian, and the smoothing parameter, b, is chosen based on the suggestion of Silverman (1986):

$$b = 0.9 . N^{-1/5} . \left\{ \min\left(\hat{\sigma}, \frac{IQR}{1.349}\right) \right\} \quad (10)$$

where σ is the sample standard deviation of W and IQR is the interquartile interval (the difference between the 75th and 25th percentiles).

Part 2: counterfactual densities. The above kernel method is used, but a reweighting factor is included. To generate the reweighter, data from two years—assume 1981 and 1988—are pooled. This allows us to generate the distribution of wages, *conditional on the vector of worker characteristics in that year.* Extending this reasoning a bit more, the density of wages at a single point in time (in 1988, in this case), $f(w;t_w=88)$, can be obtained as the marginal density of wages, w, and of the individual attributes, z, where both w and z are those obtained for 1988. Mathematically

$$f\left(w;t_w=88\right)= \int_{z\in\Omega_z} f\left(w\,/\,z,t_w=88\right)\cdot dF\left(z\,/\,t_z=88\right) \tag{11}$$

where w represents wage; $f(w)$ is the density of wages; z is the set of individual traits[3]; Ω_z is the set in which the individual traits are defined; $t_w=88$ indicates the wages are those for 1988; and $t_z=88$ indicates that the individual characteristics are those observed in 1988.

To get the counterfactual wage density that would have prevailed in 1988 if the distribution of characteristics had been the same as for 1981, the dates referring to t_w and t_z must now be 1988 and 1981, respectively. In other words, the wages would be those of 1988, but the characteristics would be those of 1981.

Assuming that the wage structure in 1988 does not depend on the distribution of the attributes, that is, that the distribution of wages conditional on the characteristics does not depend on the distribution of these characteristics, then the counterfactual density can be obtained quite simply:

$$f_z\left(w\right)= \int_{z\in\Omega_z} f\left(w\,/\,z,t_w=88\right)dF\left(z\,/\,t_z=81\right)$$
$$= \int f\left(w\,/\,z,t_w=88\right)\phi_z\left(z\right)dF\left(z\,/\,t_z=88\right) \tag{12}$$

where $f_z(w)$ is the counterfactual density associated with the individual characteristics z, and the reweighter ϕ_z is defined as

$$\phi_z\left(z\right)\equiv \frac{dF\left(z\,/\,t_z=81\right)}{dF\left(z\,/\,t_z=88\right)} \tag{13}$$

Then the reweighter can be rewritten as

$$\hat{\phi}_z = \frac{\Pr\left(t_z = 81/z\right)}{\Pr\left(t_z = 88/z\right)} \cdot \frac{\Pr\left(t_z = 88\right)}{\Pr\left(t_z = 81\right)} \tag{14}$$

The preceding nonconditional probabilities can be estimated using the ratio between the number of observations in a year and the number of observations over the two years, both weighted by the respective sample weights of the observations. To estimate the conditional probabilities, a probit is used with the following arguments: years of schooling, sex, state, age, age squared, and formal employment relationship.

Once an estimate of this reweighter is obtained, it can be used to estimate the counterfactual density by the kernel method weighted by the sample weights:

$$\hat{f}_z\left(w; t_w = 88, t_z = 81\right) = \sum_{i \in S_{88}} \frac{\theta_i}{b} \cdot \hat{\phi}_z\left(z_i\right) \cdot K\left(\frac{w - W_i}{b}\right) \tag{15}$$

where S_{88} is the set of indexes of the observations from 1988. Note that if the reweighter is equal to 1, the true 1988 wage density is estimated.

It is important to stress at this point that the counterfactual density, calculated under the hypothesis that the structure of wages in 1988 does not depend on the distribution of individual traits, must in truth be interpreted in the following form: "What would the density of wages have been in 1988 if the characteristics of the workers had been the same as those observed in 1981 *and* if the workers had been paid according to the payment scheme in effect in 1988?" At this point, it becomes clear that, with this crucial hypothesis, possible effects from a framework of general equilibrium are disregarded in this approach. Also, the changes in the premiums paid for these characteristics are disregarded.

The reweighter for the minimum wage factor is obtained by applying a slightly different reasoning, since the minimum wage also differs across the year. The assumptions made in DiNardo, Fortin, and Lemieux (1996) about how minimum wages will affect the distribution are used in this exercise:

- The minimum wage has no effects on the wages that are above the larger of the minimum wages of the two years considered. The empirical literature in Brazil indicates that increasing the minimum wage tends, in reality, to affect the entire distribution, but with greater effects concentrated on the lower tail (Lemos 2002a, 2002b; Fajnzylber 2001; Soares 2001). This hypothesis, therefore, is quite conservative because it reduces the magnitude of possible equalizing effects of the minimum wage.

- The conditional distribution below the minimum is not affected by the minimum, after adjusting for differences in the composition of the workforce. Therefore, the counterfactual density associated with the minimum wage is composed of a part above the minimum wage of 1981 that follows the distribution of 1988 and a part that is below this minimum and follows the distribution of 1981, weighted by a factor that allows the integration of these parts to be equal to 1. As shown in other papers in this report, this is not strictly true, so this assumption will introduce some bias into the results.

- The minimum has no effects on unemployment. These results are in agreement with the international literature, in which there is growing consensus that the minimum wage has only small effects on jobless-ness (Brown 1999), but, as shown in this report, not applicable to Latin America. Thus, the inequality effects will be underestimated in this report, due to this assumption.

Under these hypotheses, the wage density of 1988 conditional on the individual characteristics and the minimum wage of 1981 can be written as:

$$f\left(w/z,\mathrm{t_w}=88;\, m_{81}\right) = I\left(w \le m_{81}\right)\cdot \phi_w\left(z,m_{81}\right)\cdot f\left(w/z,\mathrm{t_w}=81;\, m_{81}\right)$$
$$+\left[1-I\left(w \le m_{81}\right)\right]\cdot f\left(w/z,\mathrm{t_w}=88;\, m_{88}\right) \quad (16)$$

where $I(.)$ is an indicator function and ϕ_w is the weighter that makes the integral of this density equal to 1, and is given by

$$\phi_w\left(z,m_{81}\right) = \frac{\Pr\left(w \le m_{81}/z,t_w=88\right)}{\Pr\left(w \le m_{81}/z,t_w=81\right)} \quad (17)$$

Integrating the conditional density associated with the minimum, a counterfactual density of the minimum is generated. This depends on the following reweighter: for wages above the minimum in 1981, the reweighter is equal to 1; for wages below the 1981 minimum, the reweighter is given by

$$\phi_m\left(z,m_{81}\right) = \frac{\Pr\left(t_w=88/z,w \le m_{81}\right)}{\Pr\left(t_w=81/z,w \le m_{81}\right)} \cdot \frac{\Pr\left(t_z=81\right)}{\Pr\left(t_z=88\right)} \quad (18)$$

Thus, the effect of the minimum on the distribution will depend fund-amentally on the behavior of the part of the sample that receives less than the 1981 minimum wage. The counterfactual density associated with the minimum wage comes from the 1988 density and changes the individual traits z and the premiums paid for these traits to those below the 1981 minimum. If this portion of the population had not in fact "evolved" over time, then the effect of the minimum would be near zero. If, on the other hand, their characteristics changed a lot over time, as well as the premiums paid for these, then the minimum will have large effects on the distribution.

Calculating the Decompositions

In performing the decomposition, the mean and two measures of inequality for each distribution are calculated: the variance of the logarithm of real wages and the Gini index. Then the difference between the measures of inequality of different distributions is calculated, following the order of the preceding decomposition. For example, in calculating the difference between the Gini index for 1988 and the Gini of the counterfactual associated with a change in the minimum wage, if the value of this difference is positive, then the effect of a higher minimum wage, given that the real minimum wage of 1981 was greater than that of 1988, would be to reduce the wage dispersion, which indicates that the evolution of the minimum in the period served to increase inequality. If the difference is negative, the conclusion is that the minimum served to reduce the inequality. Dividing this difference by the total difference for the period—that is, by the difference between the Gini for 1988 and that for 1981—gives a measure of the portion of the variation in inequality due to the minimum wage. Based on this yardstick, comparisons between the relative weight of each explanatory factor in the decomposition are possible.

The graphs of the counterfactuals are also explored to visualize at which points of the distributions the factors have greatest influence. In this case, the graphs of the logarithm of real wages are shown, since the graphs of the real wages present excessive super smoothing in virtue of the presence of outliers that have extremely high gains from work. The use of the logarithm compacts the density, reduces the problem of super smoothing a bit, and allows better visual inspection of the effects of each factor.

It is important to stress also that since the effect of each factor depends on the order of decomposition, the order of the decomposition is inverted in the estimation so as not to overestimate the impact of some components.

Data. The data used to measure the potential impacts of each explicative factor on Brazil's inequality come from the PNADs for 1981, 1988, and 1999 (September); Mexico 1988 and 2000 from the ENEU (August); and Argentina, 1988 and 1999 Encuesta Permanente de Hogares (May). The sample is composed of individuals between 15 and 65 that have some positive remuneration coming from the main source of work of the reference month. The nominal wage has been deflated by the Consumer Price Index to prices of January 2002 and takes into consideration the monetary changes between periods.

(v) Methodology for Estimating the Cost of a Minimum Wage Increase to the State: Cases: Panama, Colombia, Brazil, Dominican Republic, Mexico (Guzman, Lizardo, and Lora 2003)

Step 1: The Distribution of Wages in the Public Sector
Nonparametric estimation of the wage distribution is generated for five countries. The minimum wage is clearly binding for the public sector in Panama and Brazil, a little binding in Colombia, and it is not binding at all in Mexico and the Dominican Republic.

A critical issue in the kernel estimation is the selection of the bandwidth. The Stata standard procedure as described in Pagan and Ullah (1999) is used to provide an "optimal" bandwidth under certain conditions, but since the procedure might not be optimal in the case of a multimodal distribution, sensitivity analysis is carried out by using bandwidths 20 percent above and below the "optimal" bandwidth. The different bandwidths do not change the conclusions.

Step 2: Numeraire Effects
A plausible implication of minimum wage fixation is that the minimum wage is taken as a numeraire to the fixation of other wages. Hence, proceeding in a heuristic manner, a numeraire effect is identified if there is a recognizable "jump" in the estimated kernel density of wage at some "round" multiple of the minimum wage. Specifically, the existence of numeraire effects are examined at wages equivalent to 1.5, 2, 2.5, and 3 times the minimum wages. A certain degree of numeraire effect is detected in Brazil—where there is a bump at 3 MW—and in Colombia—where the density jumps at 2*MW and at 2.5*MW. In Panama and the Dominican Republic, there is a certain concentration of the density distribution of wages around 1.5*MW, whereas in Mexico the minimum

wage seems to be irrelevant to the public sector: it is not binding and there are no numeraire effects.

Step 3: Impact of Changes of the Minimum Wage on Public Expenditure

Two simulations of the impact of increases of the minimum wage on public expenditure are estimated. The results are based on two different scenarios. In the first, there is an increase of the minimum wage, so that all public employees with wages below the new minimum wage are adjusted to the new minimum, but there is no adjustment in the wages above the new minimum. In the second scenario, assume that the increase of the minimum wage generates an increase in other wages. Specifically, assume that the wages close to the multiples of the minimum wage in which the density function shows significant concentration are attracted to that level.

Notes

1. We also introduced interactions of the minimum wage with dummies for the first quarter after introducing legislative changes in the minimum wage in all the models estimated in the report. We found significant positive effects of minimum wage changes in family incomes in most regressions. However, we choose to present a more parsimonious specification to facilitate interpretation. The results and conditions do not differ from those pressed here.

2. Note that the fraction between the current and the past minimum wage is a "change" in the minimum wage "bite," which is the difference in the fractions of workers below the current and the past minimum wage 12 months before. These are the variables that were tested for panel unit roots.

3. The individual characteristics considered are age, years of schooling, sex, a dummy associated with the state in which the individual resides (except for Argentine data, which includes only Grand Buenos Aires), and a dummy for formal employment relationship.

Appendix II
Summary of Literature

Source, country	Question	Methodology	Data	Findings	Effect
1. Impact of mw on average wages					
An increase in the minimum wage has a positive or neutral effect on wages. The effect is felt both for those clustered around the minimum wage and those earning above the minimum (Brazil, Colombia, Mexico), unlike the United States, where the effects are confined to those earning around the mw. These results are robust across countries and use different methodologies within the country.					
Fajnzylber (2002), Brazil	How does an increase in the minimum wage affect wages throughout the wage distribution?	Regress the percent change in the wage on the percent change in the minimum wage, interacted with a dummy for location in the original wage distribution, and on other control variables.	PME 1984–99	A 1% increase in the mw leads to an increase in wages in • the formal sector (male: 0.37–1.34%; female: 0.33–1.17%) • informal sector (male: 0.09–1.29%; female: 0.27–1.14%) • self-employment sector (male: 0.18–1.46%; female: 0.14–1.44%).	+
Neri, Gonzaga, and Camargo (2000), Brazil	Are there numeraire effects? How does the mw affect individual poverty?	Nonparametric.	PNAD 1996	Spikes are observed at multiples of the mw. The numeraire effect is responsible for 6% of the wages besides the mw in the formal sector, 20% in the informal sector, and 5% of the self-employed sector. A 43% increase in the minimum wage reduces poverty rates by 6%.	+

(continued)

Summary of Literature (*continued*)

Source, country	Question	Methodology	Data	Findings	Effect
Carneiro and Faria (1997),[a] Brazil	How does mw affect wages? Is there a lighthouse effect (defined as changes in the mw that would affect all wages, even among the informal sector)?		PME	1980–1985: mw positively affected wages throughout the distribution 1985–1993: mw and market wage were determined simultaneously	+ 0
Soares (2002), Brazil	How does an increase in the minimum wage affect the wage distribution?	Kernel density plots (kdps), nonparametric difference-in-difference, and a difference-in-difference regression.	PNAD 1996 & 1999 for kdps PME for estimates	Strong spikes at 1 and 2 times the minimum wage in 1995 and 1999. Greater spikes for women, informal employees (*not* self-employed), northeast, spouses and children, no education, 16–25 years, domestic workers, black, and household per capita less than or equal to third decile. 1% increase in minimum wage causes • wage increase by 0.2% for 0–15 centile • wage increase by 0.6% for 15–25 centile • wage elasticities decreased from 25–60th centile until reaching 0.	+ for poor around mw

Study	Question	Method	Data	Findings	
Foguel, Ramos, and Carneiro (2000), Brazil	How does the mw affect other wages over the period 1983–99?	Cointegration analysis of time series.		Unitary long-run relationship (levels): A 1% increase in the minimum wage leads to a 0.1% increase in the wage for the formal sector and 0.24% increase in the informal sector wages (in the short run).	+
Lemos (2002), Brazil	How does the minimum wage affect wages throughout the income distribution?	Regress average wages on the minimum wage, with a long time series, dividing the sample by original position in the wage distribution.	PME 1984–2000	A 1% increase in the minimum wage is associated with elasticities • at or above 1 for workers near the mw, • 0.3 at the median • decreasing after and an overall compression of wages. A 16% increase in the mw leads to a • 0.6% increase in wages of the 10th centile • 0.45% increase of the 30th centile.	+
Neumark, Cunningham, and Siga (2006), Brazil	How does an increase in the mw affect wages by position in the wage distribution?	Examine behavior of the "fraction below" one year after a minimum wage change.	PME 1996–2001	Increases in wages of workers in the 20th centile among all workers, in the 10th centile for the formal sector only. Elasticity = 0.07	+

(continued)

Summary of Literature (*continued*)

Source, country	Question	Methodology	Data	Findings	Effect
Cunningham and Siga (2006), Brazil	How does an increase in the mw affect wages?	Regress the percent change in the wage on the percent change in the minimum wage, interacted with a dummy for location in the original wage distribution, and on other control variables.	PNAD 1996–2001	Increases in wages of those who are earning around the mw, with some effects higher up in the wage distribution. A 1% increase in the mw is correlated with • a 0.6% increase in wages for men and women • a 0.87% increase in wages for 14- to 24-year-olds, a 0.48% increase for 25- to 50-year-olds, and no effect on wages for older workers • an increase in wages by 0.56–0.63% for primary and secondary education, but no change in the wages of those with no school or with a university education.	+
Maloney and Nuñez (2004), Colombia	How does an increase in the minimum wage affect wages throughout the wage distribution?	Regress the percent change in the wage on the percent change in the minimum wage, interacted with a dummy for location in the original wage distribution, and on other control variables.	ENH 1997–99 (11 cohorts) Men, working 30–50 hours	Wages throughout the formal distribution are affected. A 1% increase in the minimum wage leads to • 0.16–1.74% increase in wages • the effects decrease as you move along the distribution • no effect on the self-employed.	+

Study	Question	Method	Data	Findings	
Bell (1997), Colombia	How does an increase in the minimum wage affect average wages?	Regress real wages or the minimum wage, GDP, prices, and time dummies.	Macro time series 1962–92	A 1% increase in the mw is correlated with a wage elasticity 0.37–0.44.	+
Arango and Pachon (2003), Colombia	How does an increase in the minimum wage affect wages of average workers, by position in the household?	Dynamic panel model, for each of 15 centiles, using fraction affected and minimum median wage ratio.	National Household Survey 1984–2001	An increase in the minimum wage is associated with a higher wage for workers in the 45th–60th wage centiles. No effects for the very poor.	+
Gindling and Terrell (2005), Costa Rica	Can the minimum wage affect average wages in Costa Rica?	kdps Regress wages on the minimum wage, industry variables, human capital variables, and time dummies.	Household Survey of Employment and Unemployment 1980–96	Numerous spikes at the mw and throughout the distribution for salaried and self-employed. Spikes in some industries. 21–29% increase in formal sector wage and 18% fall in the small-firm employee wage; decline of 75% in s-e wages Stratifying by full/part-time, increase wages by 26–27% (larger for big firms); no effect on part-time workers; no effect for s-e (except negative for large firms).	+, –
Castellanos, Garcia-Verdu, and Kaplan (2004), Mexico	Does the minimum wage affect wages?	SURE Augmented Kahn test. Regress the fraction of wage change in a certain range on the position in the histogram of no change, 1 minimum wage change, and less than 1 minimum wage change.	IMSS admin. data, longitudinal firms-level data 1984–2001	Nominal wage increases are correlated with nominal minimum wage increases.	+

(continued)

Summary of Literature (*continued*)

Source, country	Question	Methodology	Data	Findings	Effect
Bell (1997), México	How does an increase in the minimum wage affect average wages?		Macro time series 1972–90	No effect in manufacturing sector.	0

2. Distributional effects of mw on wage inequality
Higher minimum wages may increase or decrease wage inequality, with more of a tendency to a decrease in inequality.

Source, country	Question	Methodology	Data	Findings	Effect
Corseuil[a] (2000), Brazil	How do minimum wages affect the wages of poor individuals?		PME 1995–98	Antipoverty effects with an elasticity of 0.4 (assume no disemployment effects).	Fall in poverty
Lemos (2002), Brazil	Does an increase in the mw affect the spread between wealth centiles?	Difference-in-differences regression.	PME 1982–2001	A 1% increase in the minimum wage decreases the wage gap between the 50th and 90th centiles by 3.4%, the 10th and 90th wage centile by 5.0%, and the 90th and 50th centile by 1.5%.	Fall in inequality
Bell (1997), Mexico	How do minimum wages affect wage inequality?		Annual Industrial Surveys 1984–90 for Mexico; 1980–1987 for Colombia	Wage inequality rises a bit in Mexico, where the mw is not binding and falls in Colombia, where the mw is binding.	Rise in inequality in Mexico Fall in inequality in Colombia
Angel-Urdinola and Wodon (2003), Colombia, Brazil	How does a decrease in the mw affect income inequality?	Simulate a counterfactual distribution using wage and employment elasticities calculated elsewhere.	PNAD 1999 ENH 1999	An increase in the mw decreases income inequality. The effect is stronger in Brazil, where the disemployment elasticities were smaller than in Colombia.	Fall in inequality

3. Impact of mw on unemployment or employment

An increase in the minimum wage leads to unemployment, particularly in the formal sector. This is experienced across the income distribution, but is much stronger for poorer workers. However, it is surprising that we find such strong results across countries, since employment adjustments take longer than do wage adjustments.

3a. Unemployment

				+ (unemployment) −(employment)
Foguel (1997), Brazil	How does the convergence of the mw (and the increase of the mw in some regions) affect employment, unemployment, and OLF?	Difference-n-differences.	PME 1982–87	A 10% increase in mw leads to • an increase in the unemployment rate by 0.5 percentage points (10%) • an increase in the unemployment among new labor market entrants by 9.2% A 2.5% decline in the employed leads to • a 2.6 % increase in those who are not in the labor force • increased formality • fewer employed people in industry and commerce, more in services. +
Foguel (1997), Brazil	How does the convergence of regional minimum wages impact unemployment?	Difference-in-differences.	PNAD 1982–87	An increase of the mw by 10% • reduces the activity rate by 1 percentage point, of which 1.3 is caused by a reduction in the share of employed people and 0.3 is caused by an increase in the share of unemploy • increases the share of the inactive population by 1 percentage point • increases the unemployment rate by 0.5 percentage points. +

(continued)

Summary of Literature (*continued*)

Source, country	Question	Methodology	Data	Findings	Effect
Cunningham and Siga (2006), Brazil	How does an increase in the mw affect employment of different demographic groups?	Regress the percent change in the wage on the probability of being employed in the second period, interacted with a dummy for location in the original wage distribution, and on other control variables.	PNAD 1996–2001	Employment elasticity of −0.08 to −20. A 1% increase in the minimum wage is correlated with job loss for • women clustered around the mw (−0.25), but not men • Youth (−0.25 to −0.48), but not for any other age group • workers with primary school, a smaller effect on those with secondary school, and no effect on those with a higher education or those with no education • informal sector workers (−0.2 to −0.3) up through several mw's, not formal sector.	
Montenegro (2003), Chile	What is the impact of the mw on unemployment?	Regress change in unemployment rate, duration of unemployment on lagged values of these variables, the change in the mw, and a job security index.	Household Survey 1957–96	Increase in the minimum wage is positively correlated with the unemployment rate, incidence, and duration.	+

Maloney and Nuñez (2004), Colombia	How does an increase in the minimum wage affect unemployment in different parts of the wage distribution?	Regress the percent change in the wage on the probability of being employed in the second period, interacted with a dummy for location in the original wage distribution, and on other control variables.	ENH 1997–99 (11 cohorts) Men, working 30–50 hours	An increase in the mw increases the probability of job loss from the salaried sector, which decreases with a rising position in the wage distribution (−0.7 to −0.15). Much smaller effect for the self-employed.	+
Cunningham and Siga (2006), Mexico	How does an increase in the minimum wage affect employment of different demographic groups?	Regress the percent change in the wage on the probability of being employed in the second period, interacted with a dummy for location in the original wage distribution, and on other control variables.	ENEU 1988–98	No effects.	0

(continued)

Summary of Literature (*continued*)

Source, country	Question	Methodology	Data	Findings	Effect
Garza Cantu and, Bazaldua (2001), Mexico	How do minimum wages affect employment in Mexico?	National data: regress employment, wages, THEIL on a set of independent variables, including the mw.	ENEU 1983–2000, 1993–99	Mw correlated with higher unemployment at the aggregate level, but once controlling for time and states, the effect is less clear, suggesting that there are other factors within each state and time that affect unemployment levels.	0
3b. Employment					
Lemos (2002), Brazil	How do changes in the minimum wage affect employment?	Regress average wages on the minimum wage, with a long time series, dividing the sample by original position in the wage distribution.	PME 1984–2000	Very modest disemployment effects. A 10% increase in the mw decreases employment by 0.09%, 0.35% in the long run; same effects in the formal and informal sectors.	– (small)
Carneiro and Corseuil[a] (2001), Brazil		Time series with a focus on nonstationarity of the series.		Modest disemployment effects—10% increase in mw leads to • a 3% fall in formal sector employment in 1995 and 13% decline in 1999 • a 2.2% increase in informal employment in 1995, 15% increase in 1999.	– (small)

110

				+ (formal) −(informal)
Foguel, Ramos, and Carneiro (2001),[a] Brazil	How do changes in the mw affect employment?	Time series approach (cointegration analysis of time series) that separates the long-term structure from short-term dynamics.	PME 1982–2001	Long-term employment elasticities for • the formal sector equal to −0.001 to −0.020 • the informal sector equal to 0.0004 to 0.003. Same signs for the short term.	+ (formal) −(informal)
Fajnzylber (2002), Brazil	How does an increase in the minimum wage affect employment at various parts of the income distribution and in the formal and informal sectors?	Regress the percent change in the wage on the probability of being employed in the second period, interacted with a dummy for location in the original wage distribution and on other control variables.	PME 1984–99	Employment elasticity −0.1 to −0.3, which is stronger in the informal sector (−0.35 to −0.25).	−
Bell (1997), Mexico	What is the correlation between minimum wage levels and the relative employment level, by manufacturing sector?	Regress the share of the population employed on the relative mw, GNP, price, and time trend. Regress the number of the unskilled who are working for the mw, wages, industry variables, and time trend (fixed effects model).	Annual Industrial Survey 1984 –1990; panel ENEU 1988	No statistically significant disemployment effect in the manufacturing sector. No statistically significant disemployment effect on skilled or unskilled manufacturing workers.	0

(continued)

Summary of Literature (*continued*)

Source, country	Question	Methodology	Data	Findings	Effect
Bell (1997), Colombia	Manufacturing sector	Regress the share of the population employed on the relative mw, GNP, price, and time trend. Regress the number of the unskilled who are working for the mw, wages, industry variables, and time trend (fixed effects model).	Annual Industrial Survey 1980–87	A 15% increase in the mw is associated with a reduction in manufacturing employment by 5%. Elasticity of employment with respect to the mw is 0.15–0.33 for unskilled workers and 0.03–0.24 for skilled workers, depending on the lag structure and the exact specification. This translates to a disemployment effect of 2–12% for unskilled workers and a lower disemployment effect for skilled workers.	–
Arango and Pachón (2003), Colombia	How does an increase in the minimum wage affect employment of different household members?	Dynamic panel model, for each of 15 centiles, using fraction affected and employment status or household employment ratio	ENH 1984–2001	An increase in the mw is associated with • a decrease in the probability of employment of household heads • an increase in the household unemployment rate • an increase the household labor force participation rate.	–

| Gindling and Terrell (2005), Costa Rica | How does an increase in the minimum wage affect employment in the formal, informal, full-time, and part-time labor force? What is the effect on hours worked? | Regress employment on the mw, industry variables, and time dummies. | Household Survey of Employment and Unemployment 1980–96 | An increase in the mw
• increases formal sector employment (monopsonistic) and has no effect on self-employment
• increases the hours of work of unskilled employees, but does not affect their employment
• increases the number of unskilled self-employed, but not the hours they work
• increases employment and hours worked for full-time workers in formal firms
• decreases employment among part-time workers in large firms.
Increases employment and hours of the self-employed.[b] | + (formal, full-time) 0 (self-employed, unskilled) –(part-time) |

(continued)

Summary of Literature (*continued*)

Source, country	Question	Methodology	Data	Findings	Effect
4. Impact of the mw on the distribution of household income (income inequality)					
An increase in the minimum wage generally increases wage inequality by increasing the wages more of workers who are poor, but not the poorest.					+
Ramos and Reis (1995), Brazil	How does an increase in the minimum wage affect household poverty?	Simulated effects of a 25% increase in the minimum wage.	PNAD 1989	Secondary workers are overrepresented among mw earners and one-third of mw earners are in households with income greater than the mean household income per capita; less than 15% are in households in the 1st or 2nd wealth decile. A 25% increase in the mw implies that • Gini falls from 0.617 to 0.612 • Theil falls from 0.83 to 0.818 • P(0) falls from 29.8 to 28.4 • P(1) increases from 12.8 to 14.0.	mixed
Neumark, Cunningham, and Siga (2006), Brazil	How does an increase in the mw affect the gap between the poor centiles and the median?	Compare the minimum wage effects on household income, by centile.	PME 1996–2001	Family income for the 10th to 30th centiles declines in the long run, although the median household income does not change, implying increased household income inequality.	+
Arango and Pachón (2003), Colombia	How does a higher minimum wage affect the spread between various income centiles?	Regress the difference in income on (among others) the fraction below.	National Household Survey 1984–2001	No short-run effects, but in the long run, the gap between the 5th to 20th centiles and higher centiles increased because household income per capita increased for wealthier households.	+

Cunningham and Siga (2006), Mexico	How does a higher minimum wage affect household incomes at different parts of the income distribution?	Regress the percent change in the wage on the percent change in household income, interacted with a dummy for location in the original wage distribution and on other control variables.	ENEU 1987–99	Household income increases, especially at the bottom of the distribution. A 1% increase in the mw leads to a 0.7–1.17% increase in household income, indicating that household income inequality declines.	+

5. Impact of mw on poverty

The minimum wage has mixed effects on poverty. Studies that find that the minimum wage reduces poverty usually assume away unemployment effects. Those studies that allow for unemployment effects of the minimum wage find that these counterbalance the wage gains, leading to a zero net change in poverty or to an increase in poverty. The exception is Mexico, where minimum wages are particularly low and there are no offsetting unemployment effects.

5a. Individual poverty

Foguel et al. (2000), Brazil	What is the effect of mw on poverty (measured by wages, using P1 and a poverty line of R$50 in 1995)?	Compare poverty levels on the month before and one month after a (simulated) increase in the minimum wage.	PME 1995–98	Mw decreases the individual's poverty rates, particularly because of the effects in the informal sector. A 10% increase in the mw leads to a decrease in the individual poverty rates by 2.3 to 5.1% (4.2%, on average). (*Note:* Assumes no disemployment effects.)	–/0

(continued)

Summary of Literature (*continued*)

Source, country	Question	Methodology	Data	Findings	Effect
IPEA (2000), Brazil	How does an increase in the minimum wage affect the poverty level of the individual when unemployment effects are taken into consideration?	Simulated impacts of the mw and CGE estimates.	PNAD 1997	No effect after allowing the unemployment elasticities to enter the equation.	0
Neri, Gonzaga, and Camargo (2000), Brazil	How does a higher minimum wage translate into wages, and how do those higher wages compare to the poverty line?	Simulation of those who earn the mw and how their incomes increase.	PNAD 1996	Assume the elasticity of demand = 0. Then a 43% increase in the mw would result in a 6% reduction in poverty.	–
Corseuil et al. (2000),[a] Brazil			PME	The elasticity of the poverty gap with respect to the mw is –0.4 (10% increase in the mw results in a reduction in poverty by 4%). (*Note:* Assume the elasticity of labor demand = 0.)	–

5b. Household poverty

Study	Question	Method	Data	Findings	
Neumark, Cunningham, and Siga (2006), Brazil	How does an increase in the mw affect the poor?	Regress the centile on the change in the mw.	PME 1996–2001	An increase in the mw decreases income in the 10th to 30th household income centiles.	+
Arango and Pachón (2003), Colombia	How does an increase in the minimum wage affect the probability of being poor?	Logit.	ENH 1997–2001	Decreases the probability of being poor when measured at the poverty line and half the poverty line; increases the probability of poverty when measured at one-third of the poverty line.	+
Lustig and McLeod (1996), Asia, Africa, LAC	How does an increase in the mw correlate with aggregate poverty rates?	OLS, cross-section time series.	Macrodata 1950–80	A 1% increase in the minimum wage is correlated with a poverty rate that is 0.6–1% lower.	–
Morley (1992), LA	How are minimum wage changes correlated with poverty changes?	Nonparametric.	Macrodata 1981–89	A higher minimum wage is correlated with lower poverty during recessionary periods and higher poverty during recovery periods.	+/–

a. Discussed in Carneiro (2002).
b. In the United States, Gramlich (1976) finds that mw reduces full-time employment, increases part-time employment, and reduces hours for both groups, whereas Katz, Krueger, and Cunningham (1981) and Zavodny (1999) find the opposite.

Appendix III
Source of Data for Cross-Country Comparisons

Country	Household/individual data	Minimum wage	Poverty line
Argentina	Household Survey: Encuesta Permanente de Hogares	INDEC (Instituto Nacional de Estadística y Censos)	Government's official poverty line by INDEC
Bolivia	Household Survey	Instituto Nacional de Estadística de Bolivia. http://www.ine.gov.bo/	Instituto Nacional de Estadística de Bolivia http://www.ine.gov.bo/
Brazil	Household Survey	IPEA, www.ipea.gov.br	Ferreira, Lanjouw, and Neri (2000)
Chile	Household Survey: Encuesta de Ocupación y Desocupación de Gran Santiago. Instituto Nacional de Estadísticas (INE)	Monthly Memory, Central Bank of Chile http://www.bcentral.cl/esp/	"Social Equity/Poverty Reduction and Poverty Targeted Investment (PTI)", June 2001, Inter-American Development Bank
Colombia	Household Survey: National Household Survey (Encuesta Nacional de Hogares)	Estadísticas Monetarias y Financieras, Banco de la República; Función Pública	DANE (the Colombian statistical Agency)
Costa Rica	Household Survey	Ministerio de Planificación Nacional y Política Económica (MIDEPLAN), http://www.mideplan.go.cr/sides/economico/03-11.htm	Poverty Assessment report, 1997, annex 3, p. 40
Dom. Rep.	LFS	http//www.oit.or.cr/oit/papers/mer_trab_re p_dom.pdf	Poverty assessment, 2001

(continued)

Source of Data for Cross-Country Comparisons *(continued)*

Country	Household/individual data	Minimum wage	Poverty line
Ecuador	LFS	Central Bank of Ecuador	Only $2 /day available
El Salvador	LSMS	http://www.pridex.com.sv/mdobra2.htm	DIGESTYC, Encuestas de Hogares de Propósitos Múltiples
Guatemala	LSMS	World Bank (2002)	Guatemala Poverty Assessment, 2002, World Bank
Guyana	Household Survey	Economic Research Institute, http://www.erieri.com/freedata/hrcodes/index.htm?guyana.htm	Loxley and Jamal (1999)
Honduras	Household Survey	http://www.imf.org/External/NP/prsp/2001/hnd/01/083101.pdf	World Bank (2001a) SLC, 2001
Jamaica	LFS	http://www.ilocarib.org.tt/digest/jamaica/jam19.html	
Mexico	LFS	Mexican Statistical, Geographical, and Information Institute	Inegi/cepal updated by World Bank staff
Nicaragua	LSMS	http://www.bcn.gob.ni/estadisticas/indicadores/	World Bank (2001b)
Panama	Household Survey	ILO http://www.oit.or.cr/oit/papers/sal_pn99.htm	World Bank (2000)
Paraguay	LSMS	Labor and Justice Ministry, http://www.dgeec.gov.py/Publicaciones/biblioteca/CanastaBasica/	"Paraguay—Attacking Poverty," World Bank, 2002
Peru	Household Survey	http://www.inei.gob.pe/	World Bank (1999).
Uruguay	Continuing Household Survey, INE	INE, http://www.ine.gub.uy/banco%20de%20datos/ims/IMS%20S-M-N%20A.xls	World Bank (2001b).
Venezuela, R.B. de	Household Survey	http://www.tradeport.org/ts/countries/venezuela/ecopol.html	Ruprah and Marcano (1998).

Kernel Density Plots

Note: vertical line = minimum wage. Left curve in cumulative density function graphs is informal sector. Right curve is formal sector.

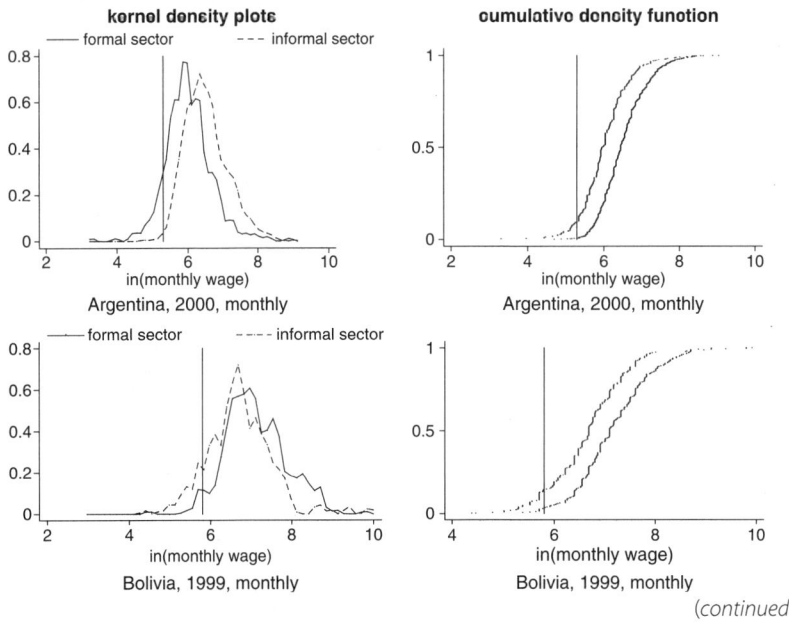

(continued)

Kernel Density Plots (*continued*)

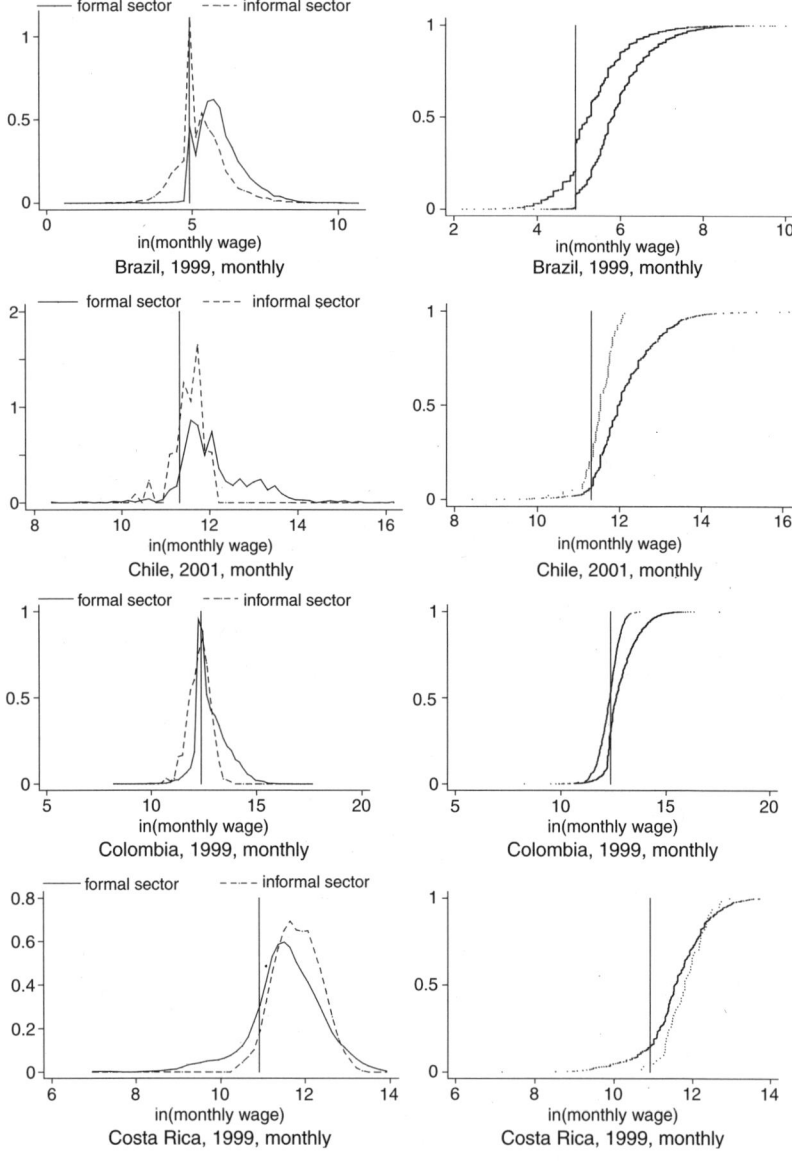

Kernel Density Plots (continued)

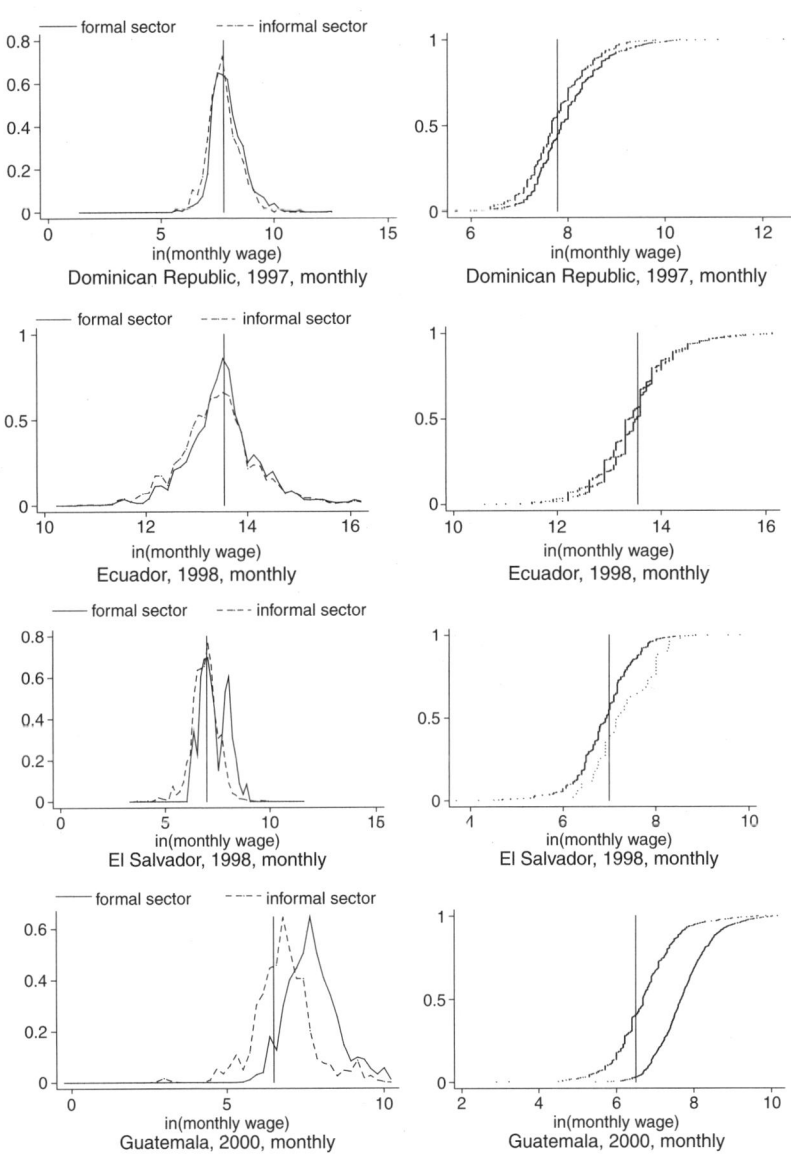

(continued)

Kernel Density Plots (continued)

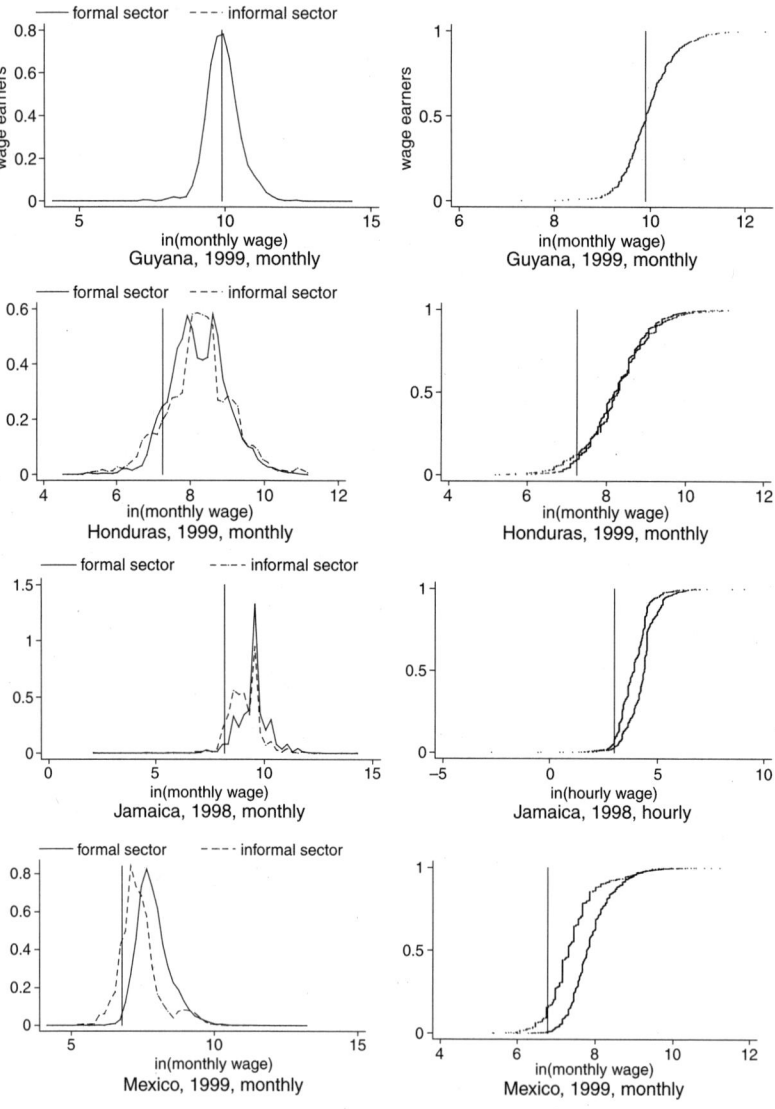

Kernel Density Plots (*continued*)

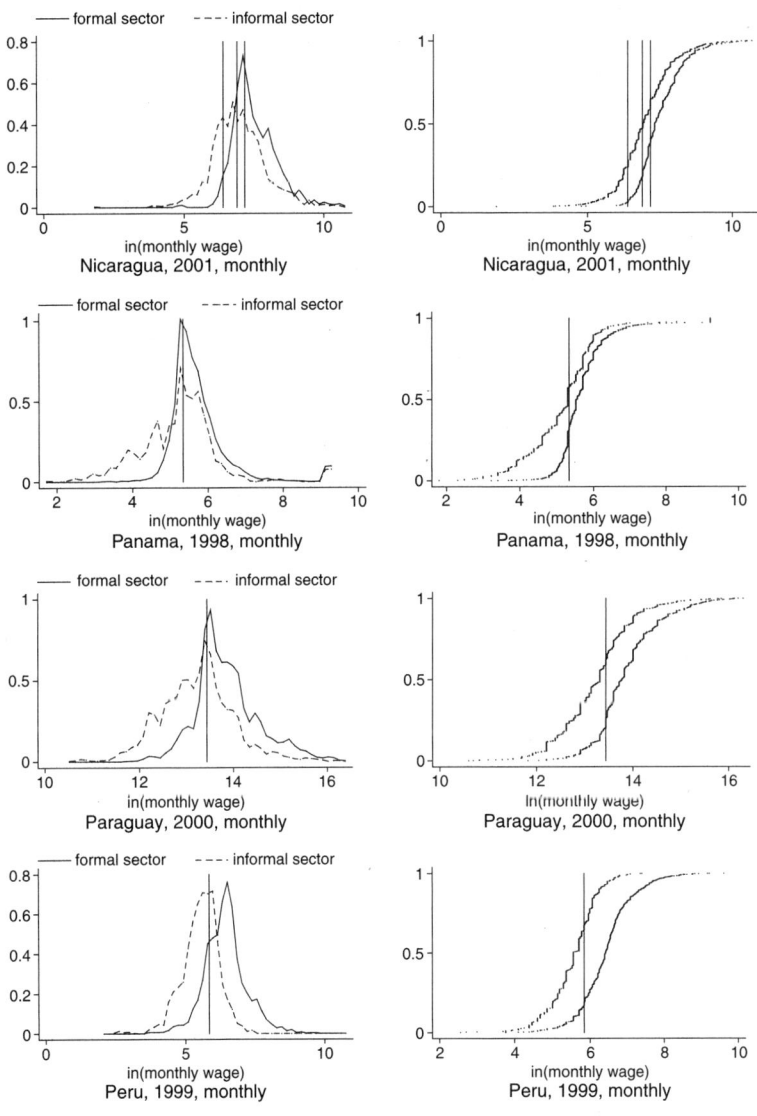

(*continued*)

Kernel Density Plots (continued)

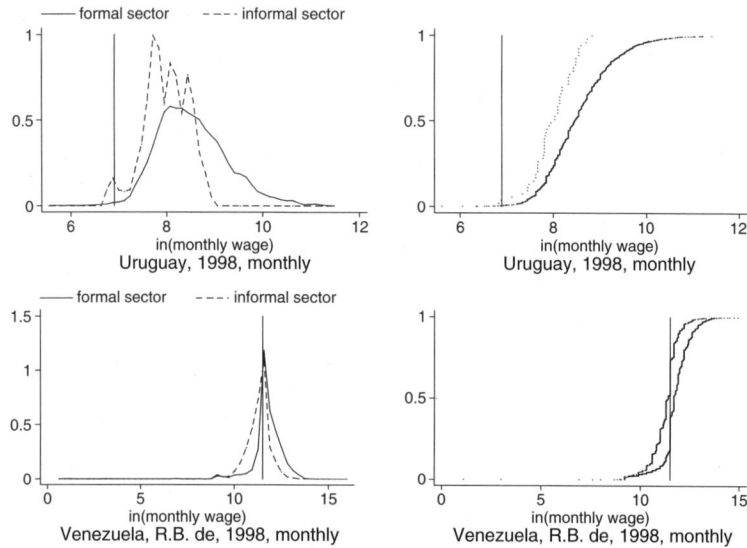

Uruguay, 1998, monthly

Venezuela, R.B. de, 1998, monthly   Venezuela, R.B. de, 1998, monthly

Source: Kristensen and Cunningham (2006).

Notes: **Dominican Republic:** The minimum wage line is for large companies. Small and medium-size companies have minimum wages that are 72 and 64 percent, respectively, of the large company level. The definition of a large company is: companies with installations or goods, or the sum of them, for value above RD$500,000 Medium-size company: installations or goods, or the sum of them, for value between RD$200,000 and RD$500,000 Small company: installations or goods, or the sum of them, for value below RD$200,000.

Ecuador: Average minimum wage.

Nicaragua: The minimum wage differs across industries. The three lines indicate the three largest industries.

Panama: Only companies with 11 or more employees are included in the analysis. Only industries with the same minimum wage are included; this means that agriculture, construction, and "other" are excluded from the density plots.

Index

Figures, notes, and tables are indicated by f, n, and t, respectively.